NEW DIRECTIONS FOR PHILANTHROPIC FUNDRAISING

Timothy L. Seiler
The Center on Philanthropy at Indiana University

Cathlene Williams
Association of Fundraising Professionals
EDITORS

UNDERSTANDING THE NEEDS OF DONORS

THE SUPPLY SIDE OF CHARITABLE GIVING

Eugene R. Tempel
The Center on Philanthropy at Indiana University

Dwight F. Burlingame
The Center on Philanthropy at Indiana University

EDITORS

NUMBER 29, FALL 2000

UNDERSTANDING THE NEEDS OF DONORS: THE SUPPLY SIDE OF CHARITABLE GIVING
Eugene R. Tempel, Dwight F. Burlingame (eds.)
New Directions for Philanthropic Fundraising, No. 29, Fall 2000
Timothy L. Seiler, Cathlene Williams, Editors

NEW DIRECTIONS FOR PHILANTHROPIC FUNDRAISING is indexed in Higher Education Abstracts and Philanthropic Index.

Microfilm copies of issues and articles are available in 16 mm and 35 mm, as well as microfiche in 105 mm, through University Microfilms Inc., 300 North Zeeb Road, Ann Arbor, Michigan 48106-1346.

ISSN 1072-172X   ISBN 0-7879-5636-8

NEW DIRECTIONS FOR PHILANTHROPIC FUNDRAISING is part of the Jossey-Bass Nonprofit and Public Management Series and is published quarterly by Jossey-Bass, 989 Market Street, San Francisco, California 94103-1741.

SUBSCRIPTIONS cost $68.00 for individuals and $127.00 for institutions, agencies, and libraries. Prices subject to change. Refer to the order form at the back of this issue.

EDITORIAL CORRESPONDENCE should be sent to Timothy L. Seiler, The Center on Philanthropy, Indiana University, 550 West North Street, Suite 301, Indianapolis, IN 46202-3162, or to Cathlene Williams, Association of Fundraising Professionals, 1101 King Street, Suite 700, Alexandria, VA 22314.

www.josseybass.com

Printed in the United States of America on acid-free recycled paper containing 100 percent recovered waste paper, of which at least 20 percent is postconsumer waste.

Contents

Editors' Notes

THE TRADITIONAL MODEL of nonprofit organizations for fundraising was based on a notion that organizations with good programs sought out donors who might have an interest in supporting them. In fact, it has never been that simple. Fundraisers have recognized that they must address donor needs in order to secure major gifts. Today, however, much of major gift fundraising is based on a different approach. There have been an increasing number of donors with ideas in search of organizations willing to accommodate them. In this complex environment, it is worthwhile to examine the relationship between donors and nonprofit organizations and between nonprofit organizations and donors.

Donors and fundraisers come together to meet multiple needs of society. Both may be committed to missions of charitable organizations, but lack of understanding of each other's roles in the philanthropic transaction can be a source of tension. Clarification and understanding of donor motivation and needs is an important step in successful giving-receiving or gift relationships. Paul Schervish opens this issue with two significant chapters on the new horizons of philanthropy that explore the material and the spiritual aspects of the supply side and the donor side of the philanthropic equation. A subsequent issue of *New Directions for Philanthropic Fundraising* will explore the demand, or institutional, side of the equation. Schervish spells out what they mean by supply-side forces, or the shape and growth of wealth and the implications of their wealth analysis for fundraising practice, the most important of which is a revision of strategies for those who are pursuing charitable gifts.

In Chapter Three, Thomas Murphy provides a framework that donors can apply in determining their comfort level for allocating philanthropic resources and uses cases to demonstrate how decisions

NEW DIRECTIONS FOR PHILANTHROPIC FUNDRAISING, NO. 29, FALL 2000   © JOHN WILEY & SONS, INC.

are made regarding philanthropic gifts. Building on the cases, Murphy illustrates how tax changes encourage or discourage charitable giving. His important hypothesis is that giving among the wealthy is more a function of expected income and expense than of current income or wealth. In other words, Murphy conceptualizes a process that the wealthy go through in determining their "supply" of wealth that they will give to charity.

Donald Ritzenhein proposes in Chapter Four a meaningful-action paradigm that is a better approach than a motivated-behavior paradigm to understand why donors give and thus a better guide for fundraising practice and research. The idea that donors seek to express their life experience by using gifts to obtain meaning is consistent with Schervish's previous work in the field that notes philanthropy is an expression of one's identity. The implications for fundraisers in their practice is to focus on donor information needs to actualize the meaningfulness sought by the donor through giving.

In Chapter Five, Emmett Carson provides an important look at and reminder to fundraisers about why the old rules of donor engagement hamper efforts in working with donors of color. Changing our traditional perceptions of donors and potential donors is an important step in engaging more donors with organizational mission.

This issue concludes with Peter Karoff's donor challenge: to move donors from a "checkbook philanthropy" to a "citizenship philanthropy." How do donors reach the transformation implied by the movement from checkbook to citizenship? A series of challenges that Karoff sets out gives us pause for reflection on not only our giving but our receiving.

Eugene R. Tempel
Dwight F. Burlingame
Editors

EUGENE R. TEMPEL *is executive director of the Center on Philanthropy at Indiana University.*

DWIGHT F. BURLINGAME *is associate executive director of the Center on Philanthropy at Indiana University.*

*Those concerned with advancing charitable giving
can feel confident about the emerging financial and
social-psychological factors that are setting new
supply-side directions in giving.*

1

The material horizons of philanthropy: New directions for money and motives

Paul G. Schervish

THIS IS THE FIRST OF TWO CHAPTERS exploring the emerging financial and social-psychological factors that I believe are setting new directions in charitable giving. These new directions revolve in large part around a shift to a supply-side understanding of charitable giving, especially by high-net-worth individuals. This chapter discusses what it means to view charitable giving from the supply side[1] and reviews the material or financial horizons that support this analysis. First, I discuss what it means to speak of supply-side aspects of charitable giving. Next, I chart the current patterns of charitable giving by wealth holders. I summarize the growing horizon of material wealth that will provide the context for increased charitable giving.

Acknowledgments: I am grateful to the T. B. Murphy Charitable Trust and the Lilly Endowment for their generous support of the research reported in this chapter. I am especially grateful to John J. Havens, whose careful empirical research is contained in the chapter, and to Mary A. O'Herlihy for her competent advice and assistance. Finally, I thank Lois M. Sherman for her courteous editorial work and my other colleagues at the Indiana University Center on Philanthropy—Dwight F. Burlingame, Patrick M. Rooney, and Eugene R. Tempel—who hosted me and provided the intellectual atmosphere that encouraged the development of the ideas in this chapter and the next one.

I then indicate some of the implications for charitable giving that such a vast wealth transfer portends. I conclude with a discussion of how this emerging material capacity suggests that those concerned with advancing charitable giving can feel confident about abandoning a scolding model and taking up an inclination model for working with wealthy donors. The following chapter explores the spiritual horizons or social-psychological factors that join with financial wealth in disposing wealth holders toward increasing the supply of philanthropic dollars rather than resisting doing so.

Demand and supply in philanthropy

All charitable giving is a relation between donors and recipients, with donors providing a supply of dollars to meet a demand of needs. The question I address here is not whether meeting people's needs is at the core of philanthropy. Both the supply- and demand-side perspective hold that dear. Rather, the question is how best to generate charitable dollars to meet those needs. The demand-side approach emphasizes that donors are hesitant givers and so must be pushed in more or less aggressive ways to separate themselves from their money. In the extreme, obtaining charitable dollars is a process of stealthy extraction at worst and shrewd persuasion at best. The supply-side approach emphasizes that donors are inclined to donate to charity and are motivated to do so by having excess financial resources and a desire to identify with and affect the fortunes of others. They do not so much need to be pushed into giving as helped to discern how to make wise decisions about their wherewithal. In a word, the supply-side approach employs the dynamics of liberty and inspiration rather than coercion and guilt to increase charitable input.

The demand-side strategy

In practice, no fundraiser simply relies on the demand-side strategy as I have described it. Indeed, fundraisers find it especially rewarding, personally and institutionally, when they pursue a supply-side approach. But the usual approach, most often motivated by an urgency to raise the sums necessary to accomplish an important mission, is to pursue the more customary demand-side approach. In order to overcome the reluctance of donors, demand-side practitioners employ a panoply of strategies ranging from cultivating friendships and presenting portfolios of needs to advising about tax incentives, instilling guilt about privilege, making accusations of stinginess, and establishing giving quotas for wealth holders. In this view, generating a positive change in the level of individual charitable giving requires that donors be pressed to shift their preference away from other uses of their money. For charity to increase, something else must decrease. In economic language, for charity to increase, donors must shift their preferences within an existing budget constraint. Accordingly, to make this shift is to be generous; not to make it is to be penurious.

The supply-side strategy

In contrast to a demand-side approach, a supply-side perspective considers the circumstances and dispositions of donors in addition to the modes and tone of appeals. The essence of the supply-side perspective is to regard changes in aggregate supply to be as important as changes in aggregate demand in producing changes in aggregate output. More precisely, it considers how changes in charitable output derive from an increased supply in capacity and chosen duty rather than from an increased demand of need and proscribed responsibility. Instead of soliciting the expansion of philanthropy by stressing exogenously originated needs and obligations, the supply-side perspective stresses how endogenous material resources and moral capacities that incline donors toward charitable giving are themselves also expanding. Charitable donations do not simply result from changes in aggregate demand or what is needed to be done. It is also due to changes in aggregate supply, or what people want to do and are able to do.

In the demand-side approach, the central problem for charities is the need to create in donors a sense of financial capacity and moral concern—that is, to convince donors they have riches to give and reasons to give them. When the supply-side approach is added, an equally central task of charities is to provide outlets for, and even compete over, what is being created largely outside their sphere of influence: an expanding material capacity for and personal inclination toward charitable giving. If the demand-side approach sees its task to get people to do what they would not ordinarily be disposed to do, the supply-side approach sees its task to invite people to participate more fully and more wisely in what their new capacities make them prone to do.

Current patterns of charitable giving

To understand the material side of the supply side requires a look at the current patterns and future prospects for charitable giving by wealth holders.

Inter vivos charitable giving

The small number of families at the highest end of the distributions of wealth or income currently contribute a dramatically high proportion of total annual or inter vivos[2] charitable giving. The 4.9 percent of families with net worth of $1 million or more made 42 percent of the total contributions to charitable organizations in 1997.[3] Fourteen percent of contributions came from the 0.2 percent of families with at least $1 million in wealth and $1 million in income; such families contribute an average of $69,000 annually. The remaining 28 percent of all personal contributions came from the 4.7 percent of families with wealth of at least $1 million but incomes below $1 million. In regard to income, the proportion of charitable dollars coming from the highest-income families is also marked. I summarize this highly skewed distribution of charitable giving by ratios of the proportions based on the Social Welfare Research Institute (SWRI) composite estimate of giving.[4] These proportions show that 25 percent of families contribute 68 percent of all charitable dollars. Even more starkly, the proportions show that 0.22 percent of families with incomes of $1 million or more contribute 13 percent of all charitable dollars. One percent contributes 22 percent, and the top 5 percent of the income spectrum contribute 40 percent of all charitable gifts.[5]

Charitable bequests

Although the correlation between wealth and percentage of wealth contributed in the form of inter vivos gifts is negative, the correlation between wealth and percentage of wealth going to charity in the form of charitable bequests made from final estates (that is, estates for which there is no surviving spouse) is positive. For final estates recorded in 1997, the average donation to charity was 14 percent. For estates valued under $1 million, 4 percent was contributed to charity. As a percentage of the value of total charitable bequests, the 0.4 percent of the final estates that are worth $20 million or more make 58 percent of all charitable bequests in terms of dollars. As the value of estates goes up, the percentage going to charity also increases. Among estates valued at less than $10 million but more than $1 million, 5.6 percent went to charitable bequests, and among estates valued from $10 million to under $20 million, 17 percent went to charitable bequests. Finally, estates valued at $20 million or more bequeathed an average 49 percent of their value to charity, 30 percent to taxes, and 21 percent to heirs. In addition, as the value of estates rises, the proportion going to heirs decreases while the proportion going to taxes increases. The one exception is that estates valued at $20 million or more allocate a lower proportion to taxes than the $10 million to $19.9 million group, reflecting the 49 percent allocation to charity.

The forthcoming wealth transfer

In order to assess the potential for growth in charitable giving, John Havens and I undertook a project designed to estimate the potential for growth in personal wealth. Our efforts resulted in the Boston College Wealth Transfer Microsimulation Model (WTMM), which provided estimates of growth in wealth over the period 1998–2052 (see Havens and Schervish, 1999, for details on the methods, assumptions, and parameters of the WTMM).

According to the WTMM, Havens and I estimate that the forthcoming transfer of wealth will be many times higher than the almost universally cited fifty-five-year figure of $10 trillion (Havens and Schervish, 1999). Our low-range best estimate is that over the fifty-five-year period from 1998 to 2052, the wealth transfer will be $41 trillion and may well reach double or triple that amount. Depending on the assumptions we introduce into the model (for instance, in regard to the current level of wealth, real growth in wealth, and savings rates), we estimate that the wealth transfer will range from a lower-level figure of $41 trillion, to a middle-level figure of $73 trillion, to an upper-level figure of $136 trillion. These estimates are not back-of-the-envelope projections. They derive from what to our knowledge is a first-of-its-kind microsimulation model of wealth accumulation and transfer. The new estimates update the figure published in 1993 by Robert Avery and Michael Rendall—and regularly cited since then—indicating that between 1990 and 2044, the value of estates in the United States passing from adults with children fifty years and older would be $10.4 trillion.

Until our estimates circulate and are reviewed and critiqued, we persist in focusing on the low-end estimate of $41 trillion. This is not because we believe our middle-level estimate of $73 trillion is unreasonably high or our upper-level estimate of $136 trillion is implausible. For instance, the $73 trillion estimate assumes a maximum real growth rate of 3 percent for the next fifty-five years and assumes that the value of assets held by individuals in 1998 was $32 trillion.[6] Furthermore, emphasizing the $41 trillion lower-level estimate with its 2 percent secular growth rate helps protect against potential charges of "irrational exuberance" arising from our not yet having modeled periodic recessions, a world economic crisis, or depression. Even the lower estimate of growth in wealth should serve to indicate the potential for substantial and even increasing levels of charitable giving, especially among those at the upper ends of wealth and income.

Projections of charitable giving

The findings about the top-heavy distribution of charitable giving, when coupled to our projections for growth in wealth over the next twenty years, indicate that the affluent will make substantial amounts of charitable contributions over that period and explain why there is such growth in the charity procurement industry's efforts to target wealth holders.

Inter vivos charitable giving

Even a modest 3 percent real growth in charitable giving over the next twenty years would mean that annual giving by these highest-income and highest-wealth families (0.22 percent of families) would move from approximately $17 billion in 1998—13.6 percent of 92.7 percent of the *Giving USA 1999* estimate of $135 billion of 1998 individual giving (AAFRC Trust for Philanthropy, 1999)—to approximately $30 billion by 2017 in 1998 dollars, or (assuming a 3 percent rate of inflation) $52 billion in 2017 dollars.[7] Even without a substantial change in behavior toward more inter vivos charitable giving and without including the additional families who will enter this group, families with at least $1 million in wealth and income in 1998 dollars will contribute approximately $460 billion over the next twenty years in 1998 dollars or $800 billion in 2017 dollars. Broadening the relevant population to the 1.8 percent of the families with net worth of $1 million or more and annual income of $200,000 or more in 1998 dollars, the potential amount of charitable giving is even more dramatic. Again, without a change of behavior or adding families who will enter this category, this 1.8 percent of the population can be expected to move from contributing $39 billion in 1998—31.4 percent of 92.7 percent of the *Giving USA 1999* estimate of $135 billion of 1998 individual giving (AAFRC Trust for Philanthropy, 1999)—to $69 billion in 2017 in 1998 dollars or (assuming a 3 percent rate of inflation) $121 billion in 2017 dollars. Over the next twenty years, therefore, we can expect that this 1.8 percent of the population will contribute approximately $1.05 trillion in 1998 dollars or $1.84 trillion in 2017 dollars.

If the real growth in annual giving by the wealthy increases by more than 3 percent or the share of total charitable dollars they contribute continues to increase even at a moderate pace, then the amounts just cited will turn out to be substantially greater. For the population as a whole, we estimate that if charitable giving grows over the next two decades at the same real average rate of 5.51 percent, as it did over the five years 1993 through 1998, inter vivos giving in 2017 will reach an annual total approaching $374 billion in 1998 dollars ($650 billion in 2017 dollars). This means that 1998 through 2017 total giving would be $4.707 trillion in 1998 dollars and $6.601 trillion in annual inflation-adjusted dollars. If charitable giving grows over the next twenty years at the average real average rate of 3.28 percent as it did over the fifteen-year period 1983 through 1998, inter vivos charitable giving in 2017 will increase to $249 billion in 1998 dollars ($434 billion in 2017 dollars). At this rate of increase, total giving over the twenty years will be $3.7 trillion in 1998 dollars or $5.1 trillion in annual inflation-adjusted dollars.

Charitable bequests

The projections for bequests are equally propitious. One apparent empirical anomaly that we discovered in our research is the negative correlation between wealth and percentage of wealth contributed in the form of annual giving (Schervish and Havens, 2001). While the percentage of income contributed increases with wealth as well as with income, the percentage of wealth contributed rises with income but not with wealth. However, the area of charitable giving that is positively related to wealth is charitable bequests. This fact notwithstanding, the value of charitable bequests hovers around 10 percent of annual inter vivos gifts by individuals. Because of the dramatic growth of wealth predicted by our WTMM, we expect that in addition to annual inter vivos giving and without any increase over the 1995 proportion of estates going to charity (something that in fact occurred from 1995 through 1997), the projected twenty-year level of bequests will be between $1.7 trillion and $2.7 trillion, and the projected fifty-five-year level of bequests will be between $6 trillion and $25 trillion. Moreover, 75 percent of these amounts will come from the 3 percent of estates valued at $2 million or more (Havens and Schervish, 1999).

In the light of these figures, I conclude that there is in fact a positive relationship between wealth and percentage of wealth contributed once we transfer our attention to the bequest side of the ledger. Although the rich will continue to contribute more in annual giving than in bequests in the immediate future, near the end of the twenty-year window, yearly contributions from bequests by wealth holders will approach ever closer to the amount of annual individual giving by wealth holders. Once again, I caution that all our estimates, in addition to being conservative, are not able to predict what behavioral changes may occur over the span of the next two decades.

Supply-side effects of growth in financial wherewithal

Despite these intriguing trends and projections in wealth and philanthropy, they do not fully take into account the supply-side dynamics that make it likely that charitable giving will increase over the next decades in excess of what I have estimated. This is because the projections assume that the relative allocation of financial resources to philanthropy will remain essentially the same as it was in the late 1990s. The projections, as striking as they may be, do not take into account the fact that increased wealth has the realistic potential to make wealth holders more charitably inclined than they currently are.

Even if there were no supply-side effect and wealth holders continue to allocate their greater supply of wealth according to the same proportions as they did when they were less wealthy, this would lead to greater amounts going to charity. But as wealth grows, individuals allocate more to philanthropy. In other words, charitable giving, unlike other expenditures, is positively income and wealth elastic. For instance, economists state that above certain financial levels, consumption of food becomes less elastic. As disposable income goes up, the amount spent on food remains relatively unchanged. This is different from expenditures for luxury goods, for instance, which are more highly elastic in relation to financial resources. But at some point, even luxury goods become inelastic. Transfers to children are generally elastic over a much broader range of increases in resources. But as we are increasingly hearing in the media and as the estate tax trends suggest, there is some point of increased resources at which wealth holders no longer choose to allocate more to their heirs, or at least begin to allocate lower proportions of their increased wealth to heirs.

That these supply-side effects are already manifested—but, of course, not proven—is clear from the comparison of the growth and changing allocations in final estates from 1992 through 1997, the last year for which data are available. For all final estates, the proportion going to charity steadily increased between 1992 and 1997. From 1992 to 1995, the value of final estates increased 17 percent, and the amount going to taxes also rose 18 percent. However, the amount going to heirs went up only 14 percent, while the amount bequeathed to charity grew 28 percent. Over the three-year period from 1995 to 1997, the shift from heirs to charity accelerated even more, so that for the six-year period 1992 to 1997, the value of final estates increased 65 percent (a dramatic finding in itself), with the amount going to taxes rising a comparable 67 percent. However, the bequests to heirs increased only 57 percent while charitable bequests grew 110 percent. The tendency to shift the allocation of estates to charity is even greater among those with estates at or above $20 million. From 1992 to 1997, the value of final estates grew 135 percent, the amount allocated to taxes increased 82 percent, and the amount going to heirs increased 75 percent. The increase going to charity was 246 percent, or 82 percent greater than the percentage increase in the value of estates.

These findings, although based on independent samples rather than longitudinal panel data, support the notion that charitable giving is highly elastic in regard to wealth and income. That is, as wealth increases, not only does the amount going to charity increase, but the proportion of resources allocated to charity also increases. In Chapter Three of this issue, Thomas Murphy examines the decision-making dynamics of wealth holders that undergird this elasticity of charitable giving. He maintains, correctly, I believe, that there is nothing automatic about a shift toward philanthropic giving in the presence of substantial financial wherewithal. One reason, explains Murphy, is that the translation of increased resources into increased philanthropy depends on the composition of a wealth holder's assets—for instance, whether the assets remain tied up in a business enterprise. Nevertheless, says Murphy, growth in financial wherewithal does result in a potential positive effect for philanthropy for households once they are at or near their desired level of consumption and when additional sums for self, family, and investment have been accumulated at the desired level. When this point is reached, each new dollar added to available financial resources is—minus any tax obligations—a dollar available for philanthropy. The essence of the material side of the supply-side approach is that it is at such a point of subjectively defined financial security that wealth becomes an even more willing ally of philanthropy. But just how strong an ally depends on how deftly fundraisers and charities can mobilize such potential financial vectors by working with rather than against the motivational forces that I call the spiritual side of the supply side. These supply-side orientations of wealth holders that incline them toward charitable giving and the implications for fundraising are the topics covered in Chapter Two of this issue.

Notes

1. I am indebted to Peter Frumpkin for alerting me to the fact that our projections of growth in wealth and their implications for growth in philanthropy are to be understood as a supply-side analysis.

2. *Inter vivos transfers* are transfers between living individuals.

3. Estimates of giving by various categories of wealth are based on the Survey of Consumer Finances sponsored by the Board of Governors of the Federal Reserve (Survey Research Center, University of Michigan, 1998). This survey counts annual contributions of less than $500 as zero.

4. The SWRI composite measure of giving supplements reports of annual giving of $500 or more from the 1998 Survey of Consumer Finances with reports of annual giving of less than $500 from the 1998 General Social Survey.

5. Our current estimate of the distribution of giving by family income is less skewed at the very highest levels of income than our previous estimate.

One possible explanation is variation in sampling. A more likely explanation is that the very large growth in family incomes in recent years has outpaced the family's ability to adapt their level of giving (in a prudent manner) to their new levels of income and wealth.

6. The wealth figure calculated by the SWRI was supported by Edward N. Wolff, an expert in wealth at New York University whose own estimate for 1999 was $29.1 trillion (Johnston, 1999). Subsequent to our wealth transfer number, the Federal Reserve released new survey data for 1998. Based on these data, we estimate that personally held wealth amounted to $30 trillion in 1998 instead of our earlier estimate of $32 trillion. A Federal Reserve newsletter (Federal Reserve Bank of Dallas, 1999) cites private wealth holdings of $36.8 trillion for 1998, 15 percent more than our previous estimate of $32 trillion.

7. Giving by families who have nonnegative wealth and who gave at least $500 annually in 1997 is 92.654 percent of total annual giving by all families in 1997. This percentage must be applied to total giving in order to derive unbiased estimates of giving by joint income and wealth categories.

References

AAFRC Trust for Philanthropy. *Giving USA 1998: The Annual Report on Philanthropy for the Year 1995*. New York: American Association of Fundraising Counsel, 1999.

Avery, R. B., and Rendall, M. S. *Estimating the Size and Distribution of Baby Boomers' Prospective Inheritances*. Ithaca, N.Y.: Department of Economics, Cornell University, 1993.

Federal Reserve Bank of Dallas. *The Economy in Action*, Sept.–Oct 1999.

Havens, J. J., and Schervish, P. G. *Millionaires and the Millennium: The Forthcoming Transfer of Wealth and the Prospects for a Golden Age of Philanthropy*. Boston: Social Welfare Research Institute, Boston College, 1999.

Johnston, D. C. "A Larger Legacy May Await Generations X, Y, and Z." *New York Times*, Oct. 20, 1999.

Schervish, P. G., and Havens, J. J. "Wealth and the Commonwealth: New Findings on the Trends in Wealth and Philanthropy." *Nonprofit and Voluntary Sector Quarterly*, 2001, *30*(1), 5–21.

Survey Research Center, University of Michigan. *Survey of Consumer Finances*. Washington, D.C.: Board of Governors of the Federal Reserve, 1998.

PAUL G. SCHERVISH *is professor of sociology and director of the Social Welfare Research Institute at Boston College. During the 1999–2000 academic year, he served as distinguished visiting professor at the Center on Philanthropy at Indiana University.*

The spiritual dimension of the supply-side analysis of philanthropy is discussed, along with the implications for tax policy and fundraising that derive from the analysis.

2

The spiritual horizons of philanthropy: New directions for money and motives

Paul G. Schervish

IN CHAPTER ONE, I discussed the general difference between a demand-side and a supply-side analysis of philanthropy, the current patterns of charitable giving, estimates of the forthcoming wealth transfer, projections for charitable giving, and why we can expect a greater supply of financial resources for charity.

In this chapter, I discuss the spiritual aspect of the supply side and draw out implications for tax policy and fundraising that derive from the analysis in the two chapters. First, I differentiate the motivational models of the demand-side and supply-side approaches.

Acknowledgments: I am grateful to the T. B. Murphy Charitable Trust and the Lilly Endowment for their generous support of the research reported in this chapter. I am especially grateful to John J. Havens, whose careful empirical research is contained in the chapter, and to Mary A. O'Herlihy for her competent advice and assistance. Finally, I thank Lois M. Sherman for her courteous editorial work and my other colleagues at the Indiana University Center on Philanthropy—Dwight F. Burlingame, Patrick M. Rooney, and Eugene R. Tempel—who hosted me and provided the intellectual atmosphere that encouraged the development of the ideas in this chapter and the previous one.

NEW DIRECTIONS FOR PHILANTHROPIC FUNDRAISING, NO. 29, FALL 2000 © JOHN WILEY & SONS, INC.

I then elaborate several inclinations of wealth holders that dispose them to make substantial gifts to charity. I address the implications of the supply-side analysis for advancing a discernment approach to fundraising and for the repeal of the estate tax. I conclude by situating the discussion within the larger framework of wealth and philanthropy in an age of affluence.

Knowing that the supply-side vector of increased wealth is linked to an expanded preference for charity among wealth holders does not yet explain why this nexus occurs and how it can be galvanized. The translation of wherewithal into philanthropy depends on the social-psychological factors that induce wealth holders to shift their financial preferences from consumption, saving, investment, and heirs to philanthropy.

Motivational models

The motivational model of the demand side differs from that of the supply-side model.

The scolding model

The conventional approach used to motivate giving by wealth holders focuses on presenting organizational or community needs to the donor, arousing a sense of obligation, offering psychological inducements, and suggesting quantitative norms for how much donors should give. In general, the demand-side strategy is to persuade wealth holders to do what they are presumed not to be inclined to do: devote their money to charity. The demand-side approach is seldom carried out without some complementary attention to a donor's intent and inclination. Nonetheless, the organizing motif of most demand-side efforts is a mode of entreaty enunciated in efforts to scold or cajole donors into making gifts. The demands of needs are presumed to be numerous and important enough, and the willingness of donors to be meager and hesitant enough, to warrant an attitude, if not an actual fundraising practice, that enlists as its allies guilt, embarrassment, comparison, shaming, and imposed obligation. The logic of this compulsion model explicitly or implicitly tells wealth holders: "You are not giving (1) enough, (2) to the right causes, (3) at the right time, (4) in the right way."

Clearly this approach has its share of highly motivated and dedicated advocates for whom it is a duty to bring the needs of others into the purview of donors and to ask for assistance. Still, when pursued in isolation from supply-side considerations, the obligation model can fall into assaulting emotions, undercutting liberty, attenuating inspiration, and eliciting only grudging compliance. The demand-side approach may obtain a gift, but it seldom creates a giver.

The inclination model

Because of the exponential increment in wealth that I described in Chapter One, it is crucial that philosophically sound and practically effective fundraising approaches be implemented. There are several specific dispositions that, when coupled to growth in wealth, motivate wealth holders to be charitably inclined. Taken together such dispositions converge in what I call the *inclination model* of charitable giving.

Instead of instructing, scolding, or even flattering, the inclination model invites self-reflection in the hope of unleashing liberty and inspiration. Rather than imposing obligation from the outside, this method elicits a sense of responsibility through a process of personal discernment. In place of the four sanctions of the demand-side approach, it proffers four questions for discernment and decision: "Is there something (1) you want to do with your wealth; (2) that fulfills the needs of others; (3) that you can do more efficiently and more effectively than government or commerce; and (4) that expresses your gratitude, brings you satisfaction, and actualizes your identification with the fate of others?"

Inclinations toward philanthropy

The inclination model does not ignore the issue of financial responsibility. According to Toner's definition of care (1968) as the implemental or instrumental aspect of love, the meeting of needs is the essence of care. At the heart of the inclination model is the question of how to motivate—rather than to deny—the relationship of care. From the point of view of the inclination model, a more profound and more effective way to generate charitable giving is to evoke and work through individual motivations and inclinations such as hyperagency, identification, association, and gratitude. The more thoroughly these forces become activated in the life of wealth holders, the more that wealth holders will pursue rather than resist the responsibilities of financial care.

Hyperagency

The first supply-side social-psychological disposition that animates an inclination toward charitable giving is hyperagency, the enhanced capacity of wealthy individuals to establish or substantially control the conditions under which they and others live. For most individuals, agency is limited to choosing among and acting within the constraints of those situations in which they find themselves. As monarchs of agency, the wealthy can transcend such constraints and, for good or for ill, create for themselves a world of their own design. As everyday agents, most of us strive to find the best possible place to live or job to hold within a given field of possibilities. As hyperagents, the wealthy—when they choose to do so—can found a broad array of the field of possibilities within which they will live and work.

When coupled to the dynamics of identification with the needs of others, self-construction and world building do not stop at the thresholds of their homes or their businesses; they extend throughout all the wealth holder's involvements, including, for those who choose them, politics, community, religion, and philanthropy (Schervish, 1997). When applied to the realm of philanthropy, hyperagency means that wealth holders, when they choose to do so, can provide enough philanthropic input to make a difference in the realm of allocation just as they did in the realm of accumulation. For example, the ultimate exercise of hyperagency occurs with the founding of a private or working foundation or with the provision of enough largesse to establish a novel direction within an existing organization, such as a clinic, endowed chair, or hospital wing. For the most part, it takes the cumulative contributions of many donors to sustain a charity. But things are different when wealth holders function as hyperagents. In that case, they individually contribute a sufficiently large donation to produce rather than simply join in the support of a charitable enterprise or one of its specific initiatives. Wealth holders not only have the resources for producing charitable outcomes; they are disposed to do so. Clearly, it is possible for charity advocates to mobilize this hyperagency by enlisting the scolding model. But it is more frequently and intensely activated by the inclination model that directly invites wealth holders to function as creators or architects of philanthropic initiatives.

Identification

The second social-psychological vector that inclines wealth holders to translate their growing wealth willingly into an expanded charitable output is identification with the fate of others. The key to care and philanthropy is not the absence of self but the presence of self-identification with others (Schervish, 1993; Schervish and Havens, 1997). Personal identification is the prototypical inspiration for charitable giving and care in general. The question for generating generosity is how to expand those very familiar sentiments of identification to include those who are relationally, spatially, and temporally more distant, that is, to a circle of human beings beyond one's kin—those who live in wider fields of space and time. Wealth holders, along with all others who engage in philanthropy, are inclined toward such identification. They do not so much need to have identification imposed on them as to have it find its expression.

Association

The disposition of identification does not grow in isolation. Identification with the needs of others arises from a nexus of contact with them. If the school of generosity is identification, the school of identification is association—that is, the constellation of formal and informal communities of participation in which donors learn about people in need and come to identify with them as being like themselves. Just as people are inclined to act on their identification with others, they are inclined to be in contact with others. People are curious and seek out sites of learning both within and outside themselves. At the same time, the world thrusts itself on us. We are exposed to reality at every moment and so are eternally and infinitely exposed to the needs of others.

Over the course of my research, it has become increasingly clear that differences in levels of giving of time and money are due to more than differences in income, wealth, religion, gender, and race. When it comes to philanthropy, what matters most is one's abundance of associational capital in the form of social networks, invitation, and identification. As a supply-side force, the desire for and exposure to association in communities of participation inclines wealth holders toward identification, which in turn inclines them toward creating a greater supply of charitable dollars.

Gratitude

In addition to identification, association, and hyperagency, additional inclinations make wealth holders' allocation of a substantial portion of the growth in wealth to philanthropy not only a possibility but a probability. One of these is the inclination of gratitude. Theologian Robert Ochs has remarked that there are three ways to take a gift: it may be taken for granted, taken with guilt, or taken with gratitude (course lecture, Bellarmine School of Theology, North Aurora, Illinois, 1969). The worldly vocation of wealth holders is embedded in the insight that they have been given much in their ascent to prosperity. For those wealth holders who are most inclined to charitable giving, I have found that taking their fortune with gratitude is the single most decisive aspect that forms their philanthropic conscience and consciousness (Schervish, 1990). They recognize that their wealth and abilities are in large part unearned gifts and that despite their worldly capacities, they are human beings who abide within a gracious dispensation. This realization in turn induces the obverse insight that those who are less fortunate are not solely responsible for their plight either and are deserving of a leg up. Religion is a potent but not the exclusive path to a more caring life of wealth engendered by gratitude. No matter how the realization of blessing develops or is enunciated, the recognition of a life graced by unearned opportunities, unachieved benefits, and ultimate contingency is at the core of what inclines wealth holders to consign their wealth for charitable purposes.

Implications for fundraising and estate tax policy

The growth in wealth in conjunction with the desire of wealth holders to make a difference and to identify with others in their needs constitutes an important positive aspect of the horizons of philanthropy. There are implications as well for fundraising and estate tax policy.

Implications for a donor-centered strategy of fundraising

For fundraisers concerned with advancing charitable giving, there is a verdant opportunity to help crystallize the philanthropic identity of wealth holders. The supply-side analysis implies that the role of fundraisers and financial advisers is not so much to create as to discover the philanthropic impulses of wealth holders. Rather than pursuing a set of strategies to get wealth holders to do what charity advocates want them to do, financial and philanthropic professionals should pursue an approach that guides wealth holders through a process of discernment by which they inductively decide how much to allocate to charity as an integral part of making broader financial decisions regarding themselves and their families. This discernment approach is more akin to a marketing than to an old-fashioned sales strategy. The goal of a sales strategy is to get consumers to do what the seller wants them to do. In contrast, the goal of a marketing approach is to provide the opportunity for consumers to choose what they need. In the case of a philanthropic vocation, what wealth holders repeatedly indicate is that their greatest need is to forge a moral vocation for themselves and their heirs in and around their financial fortune.

Nowhere else more than with the question of how much wealth holders ought to contribute to philanthropy do the scolding and inclination models differ. Many individuals and groups are challenging wealth holders to contribute a predetermined percentage of their wealth to charity. Our own research and anecdotal observation indicate that such externally declared dictates are materially unproductive. Those who impose such mandates fail to understand that substantial charitable giving derives not from meeting general demand-side injunctions but from self-ordained evaluations by donors of their level of discretionary resources in the light of their composite values and purposes.

Thomas B. Murphy, an actuary and business owner, has sought to conceptualize the usually implicit combination of financial and psychological reckoning that he and other wealth holders go through in determining how much of their resources to donate to charity. The first step is to translate wealth and income into a common denominator. In Chapter Three of this issue, Murphy argues that "wealth and income are different faces of the same underlying reality." If wealth holders are going to contribute more than nominal amounts to charity, they need to perceive their income and assets as together constituting a quantifiable financial resource stream. The second step is to understand the relationship between this financial resource stream and one's current and future expense stream. Given the generally accepted assumption that one provides first for oneself and one's family and does so at some level of lifestyle, philanthropy enters into the decision-making process when the difference between the expected level of income and expected level of expense to maintain and enhance one's standard of living is substantial and relatively permanent, as measured by the subjectively determined criteria of the decision maker. Whether this difference, as a multiple of income, is 0.5, 1, 2, or 10, it is the primary independent variable in determining the amount of financial resources potentially available for charitable giving.

In addition to clarifying how wealth holders need to conceive of their financial resources in order to view them as available for charity, it is necessary for there to be a systematic planning process that helps guide them. Fithian (2000), a certified financial planner, has developed what he calls a values-based financial planning process through which wealth holders come to define for themselves a working estimate of their resource and expense streams and make decisions about those resources and expenditures in the light of their values. Fithian's method is thoroughly inductive rather than deductive. The approach is to conduct a series of financial and personal interviews with wealth holders that result in the formulation of an alterable but specific (1) conservatively estimated resource stream, (2) liberally estimated expense stream (including gifts and inheritances for heirs), and (3) self-reflective values stream that Fithian calls the *Family Planning Philosophy*. With these in hand, wealth holders are in a position to know a self-determined minimal amount of financial resources they plan to devote for self, spouse, and family, as well as a minimal amount of planning resources they could devote to charity and to set forth consciously the biographical experiences and moral aspirations that will lead them to apply their wealth to the welfare of others.

This approach is analogous to the decision making involved in building a house. There are, of course, instances where a builder offers only one or a limited number of architectural designs to prospective buyers. But people who intend to allocate large sums to building a house typically seek out an architect who will design a house based on their desires. In this instance, a process of detailed discovery must precede the drafting of any blueprints, just as the blueprints must precede construction. For wealth holders—and really with all of us—devoted philanthropic commitments emerge from decisions that are freely self-chosen and connected to what is considered important. Practically, this means that in work with potential donors, archaeology must go before architecture and artifact. If major gifts are to be garnered from major donors imbued with hyperagency, it is necessary to treat them to the same respectful decision-making process we would desire for ourselves. This means helping donors to excavate their biographical history, their contemporary prospects and purposes, and their anxieties and aspirations for the future. Far more attention and time need to be devoted to interpreting who donors are and who they want to be rather than interjecting who we think they are and who they ought to be. It means that we enable wealth holders to uncover and carry out in freedom the wise choices that fulfill their needs for effectiveness and significance in their own lives as the condition of possibility for receiving the monetary sums that advance the effectiveness and significance of others.

Tutoring wealth holders in this method of discernment regarding both their material capacities and moral cares ends up producing something deeper than simply a more lucrative fundraising strategy, although it is certainly that. It is also a way for fundraisers and charity advocates to realize a more satisfying and effective vocation for themselves. In pursuing a methodology endowed with an understanding of and confidence in the unfolding of the material and spiritual supply-side vectors, charity advocates will find themselves contributing to the evolution of the culture of financial care in an age of affluence.

Implications for estate tax repeal

The second implication of the emergence of a new physics of philanthropy is that the customary relation or the conventionally conceived relation between estate taxes and charitable giving may no longer obtain, and this needs to be taken into account as estate tax repeal progresses. I consider that the increasingly ascendant supply-side forces inclining donors toward charitable giving, coupled to a fuller use of the discernment strategy of fundraising, will make it possible that even a relatively encompassing repeal of the estate tax will not negatively affect charitable giving and may even prove to be a boon for philanthropy.

The wealth advisement community and some philanthropic foundations and charities are, for both business reasons and a genuine concern for charitable giving, disinclined to see value in repeal, because the tax and the incentive of tax minimization are understandably seen as positive catalysts for charitable giving. Until recently, I shared this view and cited tax incentives as one of the positive supply-side forces impelling charitable giving. Of late, however, a number of considerations relevant to the discussion have led me to entertain the opposite conclusion. A review of these considerations might lead to a more enlightened debate and keep the dire predictions about repeal's devastating effect on philanthropy from being uncritically accepted.

First, the trends in charitable bequests over the past decade that I reviewed in Chapter One indicate that wealth holders are already shifting bequests from heirs to charity. From 1992 through 1997, the value of all final estates (those for which there is no surviving spouse) grew by 65 percent, the value of estate tax revenue was up by 67 percent, and bequests to heirs increased by 57 percent; however, the greatest increase was in charitable bequests, which grew at 110 percent. Even more starkly, for those with final estates valued at $20 million or more, the value increased 135 percent and tax payments grew 82 percent; bequests to heirs grew only 75 percent, while bequests to charity went up 246 percent. Another way to look at this trend is to note the growing proportion of final estates of $20 million or more going to charity. In 1992, these estates allocated 34 percent of their value to charitable bequests; in 1995, it had increased to 41 percent and in 1997 to 49 percent. There are complex forces behind these trends, and they do not prove that charitable giving will increase with the repeal of the estate tax. Nonetheless, they do suggest that the reduction and eventual repeal of the tax will not necessarily impoverish charities.

Second, with the repeal of the estate tax, the very wealthy—facing only two avenues for wealth disposition instead of three—are likely to continue to devote increasing portions of their estates to charity. In *Wealth with Responsibility Study/2000* (Bankers Trust Private Banking, 2000), 112 wealth holders with assets at or above $5 million were asked to chart both their expected and desired allocation of their estates to heirs, taxes, and charity. On average, the respondents expected 47 percent of assets from their estates to go to heirs, 37 percent to go to taxes, and 16 percent to go to charitable organizations and causes. Their desired allocation, however, was to see 64 percent of their assets go to heirs and 26 percent to charity, with taxes unsurprisingly trailing a distant third priority at 9 percent.

(Unspecified other purposes made up the remaining 1 percent.) In other words, if those respondents get their wish, their 76 percent reduction in taxes would result in a 63 percent increase in bequests to charity. The survey also showed that the desire to reallocate money from taxes to charity is even stronger at the upper levels of wealth: respondents with a net worth at or above $50 million envisioned an even greater shift to charity than those with a net worth below that amount.

Third, estate tax repeal may make it more likely that the rate of economic growth might increase once all the unproductive economic activity that surrounds estate tax minimization and avoidance is no longer needed. Economists Aldona and Gary Robbins have been reported to estimate that a repeal of the estate tax would increase the gross domestic product by $1 trillion over the next decade, resulting in the creation of nearly 275,000 jobs (Bray, 2000). This growth could be extremely beneficial to charitable causes. Specifically, the wealth projections cited in Chapter One indicate a substantial potential for growth in charitable giving arising from an increase in the rate of growth in wealth. Recall that the most conservative estimate projected that with a 2 percent growth rate in the economy, $41 trillion in total transfers and $6 trillion in charitable bequests will occur over the next fifty-five years. An increase in economic growth to our high-end projection of 4 percent over the same period would result in a projected $136 trillion in transfers and $25 trillion in charitable bequests.

Finally, the repeal of the estate tax may be the basis for a new era of spiritual depth in philanthropy—one that revolves in part around making the voluntary act of charity truly voluntary rather than a financial strategy. Here we arrive again at the social-psychological dynamics of liberty, inspiration, identification, and hyperagency—that is, the spiritual side of the supply side. Growth in wealth and the lifting of a tax will not automatically lead to greater charitable giving. But if, as I believe, the repeal of the estate tax leads to greater national and personal economic growth and generates a reinvigorated sense of abundance, voluntary choice, and care, then there is reason to believe that the trends cited here will continue, perhaps even flourish, as tax considerations fade. Instead of disagreeing with the repeal of the estate tax, charities and fundraisers might do better to contemplate how to become effective in a new environment in which contributions can flow to them—through a far less circuitous and expensive route—from donors with deeper pockets and fuller hearts.

Conclusion

I do not dispute that aspect of the demand-side approach that stresses how philanthropy is indispensable for serving people in need. However, by undervaluing and underusing the supply-side inclinations of wealth holders, those who stick too exclusively to the demand-side approach fail to take advantage of the remarkable burgeoning in the material capacity and spiritual willingness of wealth holders to allocate a substantial portion of their wealth to philanthropy. Taken together, the exponential growth of wealth, the disposition to identify with others, and the orientation of hyperagency unite to mold a relatively powerful set of supply-side incentives for wealth holders to allocate large sums to philanthropy. Such incentives, when treated as allies rather than adversaries, will provide a firmer ethical and practical foundation for garnering substantial contributions from those with substantial wealth.

We are arriving at that point of cultural passage that Keynes (1933) envisioned was commencing in his day, would be gaining momentum about now, and would come to fruition over the next three decades: "the greatest change which has ever occurred in the material environment of life for human beings in the aggregate" (p. 372). This transformation in material wherewithal opens a path to spiritual wherewithal. "When the accumulation of wealth is no longer of high social importance, there will be great changes in the code of morals," writes Keynes. "We shall be able to rid ourselves of the many of the pseudo-moral principles . . . by which we have exalted some of the most distasteful of human qualities into the position of the highest virtues" (p. 369). This new dispensation of material wherewithal will confront each human being for the first time with "his real, his permanent problem—how to use his freedom from pressing economic cares, how to occupy the leisure which science and compound interest will have won for him, to live wisely and agreeably and well" (p. 365). Human nature is not repealed but rather opened to deeper attainment. In the era of financial security and in the lives of the financially secure, "the nature of one's duty to one's neighbour is changed," says Keynes. "For it will remain reasonable to be economically purposive for others after it has ceased to be reasonable for oneself" (p. 372).

Aristotle (1908) argues that the prominent and proper desire of human beings is happiness and that in practical life, happiness derives from wise choices. The primary attribute of wealth and the most prominent class trait of the wealthy is an elevated freedom of choice in and about their personal life and their public dealings. Such freedom of choice does not guarantee that wealth holders make wise choices and generate happiness. It does guarantee that in the material realm, they have a broad horizon of choice, that their choices have the capacity to fashion the choices of others, and that they harbor the potential for making wise choices that will advance their happiness and the happiness of others. The supply-side analysis offered here suggests that we do not need to admonish so much as invite others to put behind them the spiritual confinements of the "economic problem" and take up "the permanent problem of the human race" (Keynes, 1933, p. 366): "to reap the spiritual fruits from our material conquests" (p. 354).

Those who hope that wealth holders will play an increasingly important role in attending to the needs of others, nationally and globally, are themselves at a vocational crossroads. They must determine whether the cajoling or inclination model is morally and practically more conducive to advancing financial virtue in this emerging era of wherewithal and beneficence. As more people broach the boundaries of material scarcity, they become capable of walking a path of ampler financial care and happiness. The new horizons of philanthropy coincide with the new horizons of wealth, the new horizons of financial care, and the new horizons of fundraising.

References

Aristotle. *Nicomachean Ethics* (W. D. Ross, trans.). Oxford, England: Clarendon Press, 1908.

Bankers Trust Private Banking. *Wealth with Responsibility Study/2000.* New York: Bankers Trust Private Banking, 2000.

Bray, T. J. "Why Gore Wants to Keep 'Death Penalty.'" *Detroit News,* June 25, 2000.

Fithian, S. C. *Values-Based Estate Planning: A Step-by-Step Approach to Wealth Transfer for Professional Advisors.* New York: Wiley, 2000.

Keynes, J. M. *Essays in Persuasion.* Old Tappan, N.J.: Macmillan, 1933.

Schervish, P. G. "Wealth and the Spiritual Secret of Money." In R. Wuthnow and V. A. Hodgkinson (eds.), *Faith and Philanthropy in America: Exploring the Role of Religion in America's Voluntary Sector.* San Francisco: Jossey-Bass, 1990.

Schervish, P. G. "Philanthropy as Moral Identity of *Caritas.*" In P. G. Schervish (ed.), *Taking Giving Seriously.* Indianapolis: Center on Philanthropy, Indiana University, 1993.

Schervish, P. G. "Major Donors, Major Motives: The People and Purposes Behind Major Gifts." In D. F. Burlingame and J. M. Hodge (eds.), *Developing Major Gifts.* New Directions for Philanthropic Fundraising, no. 16. San Francisco: Jossey-Bass, 1997.

Schervish, P. G., and Havens, J. J. "Social Participation and Charitable Giving: A Multivariate Analysis." *Voluntas: International Journal of Voluntary and Nonprofit Organizations,* 1997, *8,* 235–260.

Toner, J. *The Experience of Love.* Washington, D.C.: Corpus Books, 1968.

PAUL G. SCHERVISH *is professor of sociology and director of the Social Welfare Research Institute at Boston College. During the 1999–2000 academic year, he served as distinguished visiting professor at the Center on Philanthropy at Indiana University.*

Wealth holders' circumstances differ widely. The primary criterion for decisions about philanthropic giving is neither wealth nor income, because neither recognizes the prior needs of the resource owner that must be satisfied.

3

Financial and psychological determinants of donors' capacity to give

Thomas B. Murphy

THIS CHAPTER explores the criteria that prospective donors use to determine how to allocate their income among investment, consumption, and philanthropy. The benefit for donors is that the criteria can enable them to determine the resources that they can comfortably allocate for philanthropic purposes. The benefit for fundraisers is that to the extent that they can know the donor's giving capacity, they can more accurately tailor solicitations to individual donor requirements.

The first part of this chapter describes how two wealthy individuals interact with the political, cultural, and economic landscape in determining financial decisions, including their philanthropic dispositions. The two individuals are real people whose financial circumstances are widely different. While they do not represent in any way a statistical sample, their situations are illustrative of the difficulty of determining outcomes from initial decisions that must pass through the labyrinth we call the tax code.

NEW DIRECTIONS FOR PHILANTHROPIC FUNDRAISING, NO. 29, FALL 2000 © JOHN WILEY & SONS, INC.

The second section of the chapter illustrates how changes in the tax environment can induce behavioral changes among all tax-payers. This section illustrates how (1) early 1990 changes in the tax laws influenced charitable giving, and (2) the estate tax laws affect giving.

The focus here is implicitly on the top 10 percent of donors: those whose wealth, income, and philanthropy represent an inor-dinately large percentage of the aggregates. Table 3.1 sets out these percentages. This focus is not to minimize the importance of giv-ing among the nonwealthy but to call attention to the fact that their giving capacity is limited by lesser amounts of discretionary income.

The asset environment of wealth transfer decisions

The primary financial decision-making criterion for determining one's capacity to engage in philanthropic activities is neither wealth nor income but the expected current and future relationship between income and expense.

Given the generally accepted assumption that one provides first for oneself and one's family and does so at some level of lifestyle, philanthropy enters into the decision-making process when the dif-ference between the expected level of income, current and future, and expected level of expense, current and future, to maintain one's desired standard of living is substantial and relatively permanent, as measured by the subjectively determined criteria of the decision

Table 3.1. Percentage of wealth, income, and giving by upper end of respective distributions

	Percentage of Wealth	Percentage of Income	Percentage of Giving
Top 1 percent	31.1	16.8	35.7
Top 5 percent	56.3	30.9	60.7
Top 10 percent	67.3	40.2	75.5

Source: Calculated at the Social Welfare Research Institute, Boston College, from the 1998 Survey of Consumer Finances (Survey Research Center, University of Michigan, 1998).

maker. It is from this difference that the financial wherewithal for discretionary activities emerges.

The primary criterion is neither wealth nor income, because neither alone recognizes the prior needs of the resource owner that must be satisfied. That wealth and income are different faces of the same underlying reality becomes apparent on reflection. Certain assets such as stocks, real estate, bonds, and other debt instruments produce for their owner an income stream, and the value of this income stream tends to be equal in monetary terms to the market value of the underlying asset. Other assets, such as debt-free ownership of a house, reduce the level of expense that needs to be incurred to sustain one's standard of living. Still other assets, such as collectibles, produce for their owner some level of continuing pleasure that enhances the quality of life.

Once individuals have established the income stream emanating from a given mixture of income and assets, the next step is to determine the amount of this income stream required to maintain their standard of living and pay requisite taxes. That which remains is the discretionary income, which is allocated in the following ways:

- Accumulating for future contingencies (for example, through investing)
- Increasing consumption levels (that is, standard of living)
- Allocating for philanthropic initiatives

The extent to which this difference (discretionary income) between income and expense is positive quantifies the financial resources available for philanthropic activities. The extent to which this difference is perceived as permanent strengthens the case for allocating some of the resources for philanthropy. The extent to which the difference is positive, permanent, and growing in magnitude enhances the philanthropic allocation. This relatively simple criterion that establishes the amount of resources available for philanthropic purposes is within a country that encourages charitable giving but prescribes the conditions under which the gifts can be made and whose wealth holders differ widely in circumstances.

The context within which such decisions are made is illustrated by describing the situations of two individuals whose circumstances differ widely. (I use pseudonyms here.) Each of the wealth holders brings to the discretionary spending decision a unique combination of income, assets, and tax constraints that evokes a different response. Examining their decision making provides insights into the complexities that wealth holders face as they grapple with their own allocation problems. For one of the wealth holders, the decision-making process is straightforward; the decisions are readily compatible with public policy, and the ramifications for the larger community are easily discerned. The second case is substantially more complex and more important, for this second person is representative of that already large and growing class of individuals who own family businesses whose continued success and viability are important to both the individuals involved and the larger national economy.

Davis Donald is one of three children of an immigrant father who made his fortune in the real estate and construction business. All of Donald's wealth has been inherited from his now-deceased father. Except for some real estate holdings, the greater portion of his wealth is in professionally managed trusts, which produce income for Donald and his family. A significant part of the holdings is in generation-skipping trusts, which provide income to children of the donor but allow the corpus of the trust to pass tax free to the donor's grandchildren at the death of the children. The Tax Reform Act of 1986 sharply curtailed the use of this type of trust by limiting the amount of the generation-skipping tax exemption to $1 million. Fortunately for Donald, the change was not retroactive.

With no financial worries and a substantially redundant income stream relative to his lifestyle, Donald is perfectly positioned to engage in philanthropic activities. Not an activist in philanthropy, his contributions of both time and money are in response to initiatives by the beneficiaries.

Under the guidance and influence of a battery of lawyers, accountants, and trust officers, Donald is pursuing a course of decision making, the primary goal of which is to minimize the government's share of gift and estate taxes. The active part of this decision making involves a combination of lifetime gifts and bequests at death. For instance, he recently established a charitable trust partly as a way to grapple with the problems of estate taxes. The divestiture of assets will continue until it reaches the point beyond which further reductions could affect his standard of living. The bequests at death are an important part of this strategy. Donald may not be familiar with Andrew Carnegie's famous quotation, "To die rich is to die in disgrace," but he will very likely be less rich at the time of his death than he is today, and by a considerable margin.

Alan Able presents a more complex situation. He is a naturalized citizen who arrived in the United States as a young man with little more than pocket change and the clothes on his back. The rise, fall, and recovery of his fortunes are illustrative. By 1989, he had built a prosperous real estate empire. However, his assets dramatically fell in value during the recession and real estate devaluation of the early 1990s. Recently, his holdings have begun to recoup their value. Table 3.2 indicates the value of Able's wealth holdings at three points in time.

In 1989, Able's most reasonable allocation choices were to continue his investment portfolio as is or sell property, pay capital gains taxes, reduce mortgages to zero, and invest the proceeds of the sales (between approximately $200 million and $335 million) in a diversified portfolio of low-risk investments that would produce a secure income of $15 million to $20 million annually.

If Able had died in 1989, his estate taxes on $500 million net worth would have been $275 million, which would have left his heirs $225 million. If it had taken two years to settle the estate and if (in

Table 3.2. Financial status of Alan Able, 1989–1994

	1989	1991	1994
Real estate	$1 billion	$600 million	$750 million
Mortgages	500 million	500 million	500 million
Net equity	500 million	100 million	250 million

Note: It is assumed that the tax basis of assets equals the mortgage balance.

order to come up with cash to pay the estate taxes) property had had to be sold in the depressed market of 1991, the estate would have become bankrupt. A 40 percent reduction in market values of real estate between 1989 and 1991 would have produced an 80 percent reduction in net worth. The heirs, who would then have possessed real estate holdings worth $600 million, would be faced with $500 million in mortgage debt and $275 million in estate taxes, and so would have been left with a net worth of minus $175 million.

If he had remained alive in 1991, Able's prospects would have been far more advantageous, even if he had chosen to sell his holdings in the midst of the depressed real estate market. Let us say that he did sell his property to reduce debt. After capital gains taxes, he would receive approximately $70 million in net proceeds. If invested in a diversified portfolio, this sum would produce an annual income of between $5 million and $7 million. If Able died in 1991 with a net worth of $100 million, his estate taxes would have been $55 million, leaving his heirs $45 million.

It turns out that Able did not die, nor did he sell any of his properties to reduce the amount of indebtedness and the level of his risk. Like many other business owners, his life is inextricably tied to his business, making voluntary separation extremely difficult. As long as he desires to remain active in running his business, his enormous wealth will remain foundational to the business and cannot be easily diverted for philanthropic or any other purposes without weakening the underpinnings of the business. Consequently, although Able does engage in philanthropic activities in the areas of education and religion, he does so at a much lower level of activity than he might otherwise be capable of and prefer.

Although the dollar amounts are quite large and the real estate market values are subjected to an inordinately high degree of volatility during the period observed, Able's situation differs from most other privately held businesses only in degree. The problems and decisions he faces are qualitatively the same as those faced by small business owners, who now comprise 42 percent of the top 1 percent of wealth holders (over $200,000 of income and $3 million of net worth) (Stanley and Danko, 1996).

Several general observations summarize what at this point needs to be emphasized about Donald and Able. First, both wealth holders are in their sixties; death is now less remote, and it would be advantageous for them to consider decisions about managing their resources in view of their death. Indeed, one of the two wealth holders has suffered from serious heart complications in the past five years.

Second, the opportunity for philanthropy is greatest among those wealthy individuals whose holdings are concentrated in minimum-risk assets and whose income stream is stable, predictable, and secure. Third, the opportunity to engage in philanthropy is least among those wealthy individuals (such as Alan Able) whose holdings are concentrated in inherently volatile assets and whose income stream is relatively unstable and unpredictable. These situations demand the full attention and focus of the wealth holder. In effect, the wealth holders are captives of their wealth in a positive sense. As already noted, 42 percent of the top 1 percent of wealth holders are in this class. Their incomes are greater than $200,000 per year and their net worth is greater than $3 million, and they started their own businesses more than twenty-two years ago (Stanley and Danko, 1996). Few of them have college degrees. Many of these individuals have the choice of selling their business, paying their capital gains taxes, and living the good life. Why they do not sell can be captured by the lament of one who did. At the closing, a meeting that took two days and required the presence of twelve lawyers, one of the lawyers said to the seller, "You don't seem too happy, Bill. You are getting a very good price for this company. Why do you seem unhappy?" Bill responded, "Are you married?" To which she replied, "Yes." Bill's next question: "Do you have any children?" The reply again was, "Yes." Bill's next and last question was, "Would you sell one of them?" She knew without having to reply why Bill was so sad despite being so rich. In regard to philanthropy, it is difficult to get the attention of those who remain substantially devoted to raising their commercial offspring, and if you get their attention, it is difficult to get them to respond financially.

Fourth, in addition to the volatility of the income stream, the small business owner's capacity for philanthropy is further limited by the contingent liability of estate taxes. Although such tax liabilities are substantial, they do not appear on the balance sheet of an estate until death intervenes. If a business owner does not actively attend to such potential tax liabilities before death, they will, at the time of death, become potent, if not intractable, determinants in the ultimate disposition of an estate.

Able's case dramatically exemplifies the stark effects of uncontrollable contingencies (such as the tax code, death, and shifts in market value of assets) on the magnitude of one's estate and the ability of apparently wealthy individuals and their estates to make philanthropic contributions. At the same time, Able's case shows how important it is for wealth holders to face actively, rather than passively acquiesce to, such consequential environmental contingencies. For example, were he to have died in 1989, estate taxes would have extracted equity from the business, thereby reducing the enterprise's capacity to withstand adversity at the very time when its management capability had been weakened by the death of its founder. These factors, when combined with the uncertainty surrounding the market value of a privately held company, lessen to a considerable degree the capacity for philanthropy by Able and his counterparts. (In late 1999 and early 2000, Able sold a major part of his real estate holdings for cash, paid his capital gains taxes, and has substantially increased his philanthropic activities in the areas of education and religion while continuing an active engagement in his business.)

Tax laws, behavioral effects, and philanthropy

Now consider how the interaction between the tax and wealth environments affects the level of philanthropic giving. That is, to understand the effect of tax provisions on philanthropic giving, it is necessary to explore how tax laws first change people's financial decision making and how such changes influence philanthropic giving. I propose a three-variable model as a starting point:

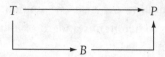

where T is a tax provision, B is a set of behavioral effects produced by the tax provision, and P is philanthropic contributions in dollars.

This model postulates that tax provisions have a direct effect on philanthropic contributions, independent of any additional behavioral changes the tax provision may induce. That is, even those who ignore or avoid the potential behavioral effects of changes in tax provisions are required to act within the constraints of tax provisions in deducting philanthropic contributions.

The model also indicates that the effect of tax provisions on philanthropic giving is mediated by specific behavioral effects. That is, the tax provision provides an array of incentives and disincentives that changes the behavior of individuals and, hence, the economic capacity to give to charity. There are four effects that we will consider here:

B_1, an income effect
B_2, a price effect, or cost-of-giving effect
B_3, a composition effect
B_4, a wealth effect

The effect on capacity to give depends on the characteristics of the tax (tax rates and the types of assets affected) and the tax-induced behavioral changes, especially those made by the wealth holders who actively, rather than passively, respond to the tax changes. This is illustrated by two changes that were incorporated in the tax code passed by the Congress and signed by the president in 1993: an increase in the top marginal income tax rate and the charitable deduction for appreciated property.

Income and price effects

Theoretically, one's capacity to engage in philanthropic activity can be captured by the following index: capacity to give is equal to income, less taxes and less expenses, to maintain standard of living divided by expenses to maintain standard of living. Expressed symbolically,

$$Cg = \frac{Y - T - SLe}{SLe}$$

where Cg is the capacity to give, Y is income, T is taxes, and SLe is expenses to maintain one's standard of living.

The 1991 and 1993 tax law changes increased the marginal income tax rate on individual incomes greater than $250,000 from 31.0 percent to 39.6 percent, an increase of 27.7 percent. For both Donald and Able, the increases in marginal income tax rates decrease the potential capacity to give by an amount precisely equal to the amount transferred by way of the tax increase from the individuals to the government. This is an expression of the negative income effect. Therefore, before the 27.7 percent increase in marginal income tax rates,[1] the capacity to give was greater because any wealthy individual paying taxes at the tax rate would have been left with 8.6 percent more of the discretionary income taxed at the maximum rate. Expressed symbolically,

$$Cg \text{ (at time 1)} = \frac{Y - .31(Y) - SLe}{SLe}$$

while
$$Cg \text{ (at time 2)} = \frac{Y - .396(Y) - SLe}{SLe}$$

At the same time, every change in marginal income tax rates also changes the cost of giving, or what amounts to the psychological capacity to give. That is, every increase in marginal income tax rates that produces a negative income effect also produces a countervailing positive price effect, reducing the cost of giving. As marginal income tax rates increase, the additional amount of discretionary income that a donor must contribute to determine the social use of a dollar decreases. For example, a marginal income tax rate of 31 percent means that for every philanthropic dollar that donors choose to direct, it costs the donors 69.0 cents and the government 31.0 cents. However, with a marginal income tax rate of 39.6 percent, every dollar of philanthropy costs the donor 60.4 cents and the government 39.6 cents.

Because the price and income effects interact with each other in opposite directions and with the other effects I will discuss, and because of potential additional changes in the cultural environment and motivational situation of donors, it is difficult to predict the long-term effects on charitable giving. For instance, while the changes in marginal income tax rates encourage giving by reducing the cost (or price) of making a gift from 69.0 percent to 60.4 percent, the same changes discourage giving by reducing the amount of donors' discretionary income. Fortunately, the third variable in the preceding formula provides a hint about how to determine the relative impact of the income and price effects. By taking into account the degree to which a new income tax schedule impinges on a wealth holder's customary standard of living, we can begin to estimate how consequential the negative income effect may be. For instance, a high capacity-to-give index, say at 5, indicates a high degree of redundancy in the donor's capacity to give; therefore, the donor is less likely to alter his giving pattern. If the capacity-to-give index is at or below 1, then the income effect is more likely to reduce his giving. Intuitively, this means that wealthy individuals who lose a greater amount of their discretionary income because of an increase in marginal income tax rates will reduce their giving more than will the superwealthy, whose income stream is relatively less affected. For instance, we would expect small business owners who have a greater proportion of their assets as foundational to their business to be especially sensitive to such negative income effects. In contrast, for wealth holders whose cash flow is derived from tax-free bonds or generated from real estate depreciation, the income effect on capacity to give is less significant and could be negligible.

The second 1993 tax change permitted a charitable deduction equal to the fair market value for gifts of appreciated property made to qualified charitable organizations. The difficulty in obtaining valid evaluations for appreciated property, particularly with respect to works of art, led lawmakers in 1986 to rescind the provision that allowed deductions to be determined by current market value of the appreciated assets. The 1993 change allows the donor to receive not only a deduction for the original cost of the gift but for whatever appreciation may have occurred since the donor acquired the asset.

This provision also affects charitable giving by a price and an income effect. But in this case, not only is the price effect extremely positive, but the effect on the donor's cash flow is positive as well. The behavioral effect should be a short-term increase in gifts of appreciated property and a sustained higher level over the long term. For example, let us consider a gift of a work of art or restricted stock with a current market or appraised value of $100,000 and a cost basis of $10,000. Subject to annual limitations, this gift now provides the donor a $100,000 deduction, or a reduction in taxes of $39,600 (at 1993 top bracket of 39.6 percent), versus the situation prior to the change, which provided a deduction of $10,000 and a reduction in taxes of $3,100 (at the pre-1993 top bracket of 31 percent). In addition, when capital gains tax savings are taken into account, the cost is reduced even further, to just $35,200 ($100,000 less 28 percent capital gains tax on $90,000, which equals $74,800 less the income tax deduction of $39,600, or $35,200).[2] Prior to the change, the net cost to the donor would have been $71,700 ($74,800 minus $3,100). Thus, the tax change produced a reduction in the cost of giving this type of asset by 49 percent, increasing the donor's cash flow by $49,000. For those with such assets, this change provides the opportunity not only to make a significant contribution of a non-income-producing asset at a relatively low cost but also to convert the reduction in taxes into a positive cash flow. Given these calculations, we can confidently predict that an increase in donations of this type of asset will occur.

The liquidating effect

People's capacity for philanthropy cannot be defined without reference to the liquidity of their assets (that is, the relative amount of wealth invested in various types of assets, such as real estate, stocks, bonds, cash, collectibles, and privately held small businesses) and the flexibility to shift or redistribute wealth among the various asset holdings as their needs change or in response to changes in the tax code.

The composition of a particular individual's assets reflect his or her preferences based on the characteristics of assets with respect to safety, liquidity, and yield. With the exception of privately held small businesses, individuals allocate their wealth in pursuit of some or all of the following objectives:

- Preservation of capital or safety
- Payments from assets
- Growth of capital to increase wealth
- Deployment for philanthropic purposes

Both income and estate tax provisions influence these allocations. For example, an allocation that pursues growth may limit one's capacity for philanthropy in the short run while enhancing it in the long run. As I already noted, the cost of allocating assets for philanthropy depends not only on the asset but on whether and how one owns it—for example, as appreciated stock, collectibles, or retirement accounts.

With respect to wealth stored within the structure of a small business, little, if any, flexibility may be present because the wealth is foundational to the business and may not be able to be withdrawn without jeopardizing the health of the business. Frequently capitalized at levels that constrain growth, these entities provide the job-creating growth that fuels the larger economy. The capital requirements of these businesses, when combined with their relative inflexibility to reallocate assets in response to changes in the tax code, might sharply curtail the philanthropic activities of their owners.

Although small businesses are limited in their ability to respond to changes in the tax code, they do respond when they can and pay additional taxes when they cannot, as the following two instances illustrate. When the tax law made it more advantageous to pay taxes at individual rates rather than at the higher corporate rates, the number of businesses that switched their tax-paying status to "Subchapter S" increased from 257,475 in 1970, to 545,389 in 1980, and 1,575,092 in 1990. Conversely, changes increased marginal income tax rates for individual taxpayers and Subchapter S corporations from 28 percent to 31 percent in 1991 and to 39.6 percent in 1993. These increases had the effect of channeling what would be additional capital available for investment from small businesses to the government.

Fundraisers need to be aware that the substantial repositories of wealth stored within small businesses may be limited in their availability for philanthropic purposes.

The wealth effect

The fourth behavioral effect of tax laws concerns implications of estate tax laws for wealth transfer. The wealth effect is the behavioral response induced by tax provisions that affect both the short- and long-term capacity to give by encouraging or discouraging growth in individual wealth levels. How an individual wealth holder responds to tax provisions depends on his or her income and wealth levels relative to his or her economic needs. For the overwhelming majority of Americans, their level of wealth accumulation is somewhat below that which they desire, and so they are motivated to increase their wealth through the investment of savings. For this large segment of the population, the motivation to increase their wealth holdings will most likely be more powerful and controlling than their efforts to minimize the adverse effects of tax changes. Large in numbers but with limited wealth, this group will pursue economic goals that are compatible with what has been the expressed national economic goal—increasing gross domestic product (GDP)—ever since John Maynard Keynes first theorized, during the depths of the Great Depression, that increasing GDP was the most important factor in producing job growth.

For a small but rapidly growing number of the wealthy who control in the aggregate an inordinately large percentage of the nation's wealth, their existing levels of wealth are equal to or in excess of their current and future economic needs. While in 1997 only 2.2 percent of families had sufficient wealth to be subject to the estate tax provisions of the tax code, projections by Havens and Schervish (1999) show that in the twenty-year period ending in 2017, 6.5 percent of the 25.8 million final estates will owe an estate tax, even taking into account the rise in the asset requirement. According to calculations by the Boston College Social Welfare Research Institute, the top one-half of 1 percent of the population owns 25.7 percent of total wealth (Survey Research Center, University of Michigan, 1998). Currently, most estimates place total wealth in excess of $30 trillion. It is in this area that income and estate tax laws interact with the personal motivations of the wealthy to encourage the allocation of assets in ways that are inimical to a national objective of providing job-creating economic growth. When the rewards associated with successful risk-taking entrepreneurial activities are taxed at such high levels (income at a marginal rate of 39.6 percent, capital gains at 20 percent, and gift and estates at 55 percent) and the losses associated with unsuccessful ventures are borne 100 percent by the investor, some owners of excess capital may be dissuaded from pursuing such ventures. The result is that such capital flows into safe wealth-preserving assets rather than job-producing growth ventures.

These effects enter into the decision making of both those whose wealth is deployed in instruments easily transferable and those whose wealth is encased in small family businesses. These effects become clearer in contemplating the explicit conflict that is present when one considers the purpose of government economic policy (to increase GDP) juxtaposed against the purposes of both groups of wealthy. The purpose of those whose wealth is readily transferred among alternative investment vehicles is all too often preservation of capital and transfer to the next generation, as opposed to growth of capital, for the obvious reason that they have enough capital for their needs. The responses among this group to the estate tax laws are, to an increasing degree, taking several forms:

- Increasing inter vivos (while living) transfers
- Removing assets to offshore tax havens outside the jurisdiction of the taxing authorities
- Changing the status of one's citizenship to that of a country with lower estate taxes
- Allocating funds for philanthropic purposes

There has been an increase in the number and amounts of very large donations, as well as a persistent increase in overall levels of giving.

Among those whose wealth is encased in family businesses, the area in which greater job growth takes place, the responses take the following forms:

- Eschewing the risk of taking the enterprise to the next level—for example, expanding from a city operation to a statewide operation, from a statewide operation to a regional or national operation, or from a national to an international or global operation.
- Focusing the attention of the business on presenting to the government a set of financial numbers that minimizes the valuation of the businesses for estate tax purposes. Extracting 55 percent of the equity of many capital-short small businesses for estate taxes, for example, creates inordinately leveraged companies.[3]

I can only hint at the complexities that confront individual wealth holders as they attempt to achieve their objectives by allocating their "free" resources among investments, additional consumption, and philanthropy. For both individual wealth holders and those fundraisers who assist them as they pursue their goals in the ever changing environment, a clear understanding of the landscape in which they dwell will help them to reach their objectives.

Conclusion

Long-term trends in the United States have been evidenced by a persistent rise in national income as measured by GDP and a concomitant increase in accumulated wealth. The growth in GDP has produced for the most part an increase in discretionary income at all levels. At the lower- and middle-income levels, the increases in disposable income have been properly used to increase the living standards of those who received them. At the upper-income levels, the limitations for consumption create an unusually fertile area for the allocation of amounts of discretionary income for philanthropic purposes. This phenomenon, combined with the burgeoning number of people entering the wealthy class, defines a growing potential for philanthropy that could justify Schervish's prediction that we are entering a golden age of philanthropy.

Notes

1. Marginal tax rates as opposed to average tax rates are used to simplify the illustration. In addition, wealth holders tend to make decisions based on marginal tax rates.
2. The capital gains tax rate currently is 20 percent.
3. The effects cited in the preceding sections reflect what an unscientific sample of residents of a small but wealthy community have done over the most recent fourteen-year period. These effects cannot be projected to the entire population of the wealthy.

References

Havens, J. J., and Schervish, P. G. *Millionaires and the Millennium: The Forthcoming Transfer of Wealth and the Prospects for a Golden Age of Philanthropy.* Boston: Social Welfare Research Institute, Boston College, 1999.

Stanley, T. J., and Danko, W. D. *The Millionaire Next Door.* Marietta, Ga.: Longstreet Press, 1996.

Survey Research Center, University of Michigan. *Survey of Consumer Finances.* Washington, D.C.: Board of Governors of the Federal Reserve, 1998.

THOMAS B. MURPHY *is the major benefactor of the Thomas B. Murphy Foundation Charitable Trust, a private foundation. For the past ten years, he has been actively involved in philanthropic research projects conducted by the Social Welfare Research Institute at Boston College.*

Motivation is an incomplete explanation of what it means to be a donor. People are engaged in a search for meaning, and they give to help achieve one or more of their needs for meaning.

4

One more time: How do you motivate donors?

Donald N. Ritzenhein

IN HIS NOW-CLASSIC ARTICLE, "One More Time: How Do You Motivate Employees?" Herzberg (1987) summarized his motivation-hygiene theory of job satisfaction. Herzberg had discovered that the motivation to perform on the job comes from within and is a function of the meaning that our job has for us. Intrinsic meaning, rather than external threat or inducement, is the real source of the motivation to succeed. External threats or inducements, which Herzberg called "hygiene factors," contribute to job dissatisfaction but not to job satisfaction. Herzberg identified the internal sources of meaning for work that result in satisfaction as "achievement, recognition for achievement, the work itself, responsibility, and growth or advancement" (p. 2). Just as the chapters in this issue of *New Directions for Philanthropic Fundraising* examine the changing dynamics of fundraising from donors' perspectives, Herzberg was able to identify the internal sources of motivation by looking at work from the perspective of workers, not employers.

Herzberg's identification of the factors that create meaning in work mirror a broader set of factors that Baumeister (1991) has

NEW DIRECTIONS FOR PHILANTHROPIC FUNDRAISING, NO. 29, FALL 2000 © JOHN WILEY & SONS, INC.

identified as contributing to our overall sense of meaning in life. After conducting a cross-disciplinary review of a large body of research and scholarship on meaning, Baumeister concludes that we possess an innate need for meaning in our lives. More specifically, he proposes that we have four needs for meaning: a need for purpose (achieving goals), a need for value (justifying our actions as being good), a need for efficacy (control over events), and a need for self-worth. The parallels to Herzberg's work are clear: Baumeister's purpose equates to Herzberg's achievement, value equates to the work itself, efficacy equates to responsibility, and self-worth equates to recognition and growth. Baumeister concludes that we are motivated to engage in behaviors that are meaningful, which help us fulfill a sense of meaning in our lives.

If meaning is a major source of motivation in life and work, it would seem likely that meaning might also be a major source of motivation for giving. I am suggesting here that donors are indeed motivated to give when giving is meaningful for them. Unfortunately, we have not seen this as clearly as we might because we accept, without serious challenge, a "motivated behavior" paradigm, which defines why donors give and in turn guides our fundraising practice and research. I will discuss this paradigm and its shortcomings, then propose an alternative "meaningful action" paradigm. Evidence for this alternative paradigm comes from a research study on information needs that I conducted among alumni donors to Wayne State University and whose findings I report here. I conclude by suggesting that a meaningful action paradigm is also supported by some other fundraising research, and I outline some of the implications of this new paradigm for practicing fundraisers.

The motivated behavior paradigm

Kuhn (1970) describes a paradigm as "the entire constellation of beliefs, values, techniques, and so on shared by members of a given community" and the related group of "puzzle-solutions" that emerge from that constellation (p. 175). Although Kuhn wonders whether the social sciences have acquired paradigms at all, there appear to be constellations of beliefs, values, and techniques that are shared by the fundraising community and provide ways of looking at, answering, and acting on our common challenge to raise private support for our institutions or causes. I suggest that motivation is one of those paradigms.

In a response to questioning about why they thought donors give, fundraisers listed twenty "motivations"—an eclectic mix of reasons ranging from "marketing" and "image" to "enjoyment" and "empathy" (Mutz and Murray, 2000, pp. 126–127). Not only do fundraisers see donors' behavior as motivated, donors themselves, even as they describe the rich background against which their philanthropy is carried out, are caught up in the motivational paradigm as "they acknowledge the more dubious motives behind some contributions and the importance of appealing to these in fundraising" (Ostrower, 1995, p. 129). As a result of what we see and what we believe about donors or prospective donors, we act toward them in ways consistent with our motivated behavior paradigm. Perhaps not all fundraisers would share Seymour's (1988) contention that "people respond to rewards and recognition somewhat like performing seals and white mice" (p. 103), but many would accept Myers's (1992) conclusion that "it is well-known that past donors who have been properly thanked are every institution's best prospects for future gifts" (p. 105). Few fundraisers, if any, would find fault with Schneiter's (1985) advice: "To succeed in fundraising, you must acquire a working knowledge of the *forces that motivate people to give*" (p. 15, emphasis added).

Motivation refers "mainly to an inner urge that moves or prompts a person to action, though it may also apply to a contemplated result, the desire for which moves the person" (*Random House Dictionary*, 1979, p. 6). The paradigm that emerges from a fundamental focus on motivation as the cause of donor behavior relies on four assumptions:

1. Individuals possess internal psychological "entities" (Campbell, 1996, p. 190)—attitudes, emotions, beliefs, desires, values, interests—that can cause them to make a donation.

2. These internal entities are preexisting conditions, held prior to giving.

3. Soliciting a gift involves stimulating these internal, preexisting entities through rational and emotional appeals. (Cialdini, 1984, provides a full discussion of the triggering mechanism of motivation.)

4. When these internal, preexisting entities are successfully stimulated and a gift is made, the task of fundraisers is to reward donors through acknowledgment, recognition, and feedback.

The motivated behavior paradigm is a mechanistic, stimulus-response-reward model of human activity. My argument, supported by the results of the information need research reported here, is not that motivation, understood as the response to an external stimulus, does not exist as a factor in gift-making decisions, but that motivation is an incomplete explanation of what it means to make a gift, and an especially incomplete explanation of what it means to be a donor. People are engaged in a search for meaning, and giving, over time or in significant amounts, occurs when it helps people achieve one or more of their needs for meaning. In order for a person to make a charitable contribution, motivation, understood as a source of energy to respond to an appeal, may be necessary, but it is not sufficient. This lack of sufficiency is borne out in study after study in a futile search for the magic bullet of motivated giving (Kelly, 1997). If we want to limit our objectives to raising money, then motivational strategies have offered, and can continue to offer, techniques that work on some people. But if we want to recruit donors, and even to experience greater success with individual acts of giving, we need to go beyond the limits of motivated behavior to the broader concept of meaningful action.

An alternative paradigm: Meaningful action theory

The concept of meaning may be, as Means (2000) suggests, "seriously undertheorized" (p. 578). Nevertheless, meaning has been a subject of scholarly and research interest in many social science disciplines, including psychology, linguistics, sociology, philosophy, communication, anthropology, and history. Viktor Frankl is the founder of the modern focus on meaning in psychology. He began thinking about the role of meaning in life before World War II. During the war, he confirmed his theories as he marveled at the lengths to which his fellow concentration camp prisoners went to maintain human dignity and survive (Barnes, 1998). After the war, he developed a specific method for helping people lead happy, meaningful lives, which he called *logotherapy*. Logotherapy deviated from psychoanalysis by ascribing a "will to meaning" as a fundamental force of human action (Frankl, 1984). Since Frankl's initial publications, a critical mass of research and opinion has emerged that confirms the existence of and importance of meaning, "not only for survival but also for health and well-being" (Wong and Fry, 1998, p. xvii). Baumeister (1991) is among those whose research supports the centrality of meaning in people's lives.

Although theorizing may still be incomplete, there is sufficient evidence to support the following assumptions of a meaningful action theory of giving:

- Individuals possess an inherent predisposition, or need, for meaning, and they make donations to the extent that doing so is, or is expected to be, meaningful to them (Baumeister 1991).
- The meaning of giving is retrospective; it is fully experienced only after a gift or gifts have been made.
- If they operate within a meaningful action paradigm, fundraisers will not "solicit gifts" so much as they will "recruit donors." Except for extraordinarily large gifts, the meaningfulness of giving will likely come not from a single gift but from the ongoing experience of giving—of defining oneself as a donor.
- When individuals decide to become donors, the fundraiser's task is to manage the meaning of giving for them.

One way to identify whether donor action is motivated by meaning, and to uncover what that meaning might be, is to try to understand giving from the perspective of a donor. Although most research studies bluntly ask donors, in one form or another, "Why did you give?" a better way to uncover meaning is to conduct an information-needs study, which is what I did, and whose findings lend support to a meaningful action theory of giving.

The information needs of donors

Dervin (1983) found that information needs exist when individuals confront gaps between what they know and what they want to know, or between what they can do and what they want to do, and when these gaps can be filled by what these individuals would call information. Given the exploratory nature of my research, I chose to use a conventional definition of information: information is "what we know; we think of [it] in terms of meaning" (Infante, Rancer, and Womack, 1993, p. 124). Even conventionally, we can describe two specific characteristics of information: content and properties. When we think of conveying information, we are usually focusing on the content feature of information (Watzlawick, Beavin, and Jackson, 1967). Content is the *what* of information—the matter dealt with. In addition to content, there are property features of information. Information does not just happen; it comes (or not) at a given time and with a given frequency, it is complete or incomplete to a certain degree, it is easy or hard to obtain, it has a degree of accuracy or inaccuracy, it comes in a certain form, and it possesses a degree of relevance or irrelevance to a potential recipient (Senn, 1979).

The information-needs study

This study of information needs examined both the content and the properties of information and asked the research question, "What are the information needs of donors?" The study was conducted in a qualitative phase and a quantitative phase. The qualitative phase identified the information needs of donors that surfaced during focus group interviews of alumni donors to Wayne State University. The interviews were conducted by an independent research firm (AFFINA in Troy, Michigan), were videotaped and transcribed, and were content-analyzed using established techniques for such research. Results of the focus group were used both to understand donors' information needs and to construct a questionnaire, which was mailed to a stratified sample of alumni donors to Wayne State University. (For a complete discussion of methodology, see Ritzenhein, 1991.)

Focus groups

This study assumed at a minimum that information has both content and property dimensions. As alumni donors expressed their needs for information in the focus groups, their comments supported this view of information.

Alumni donors spoke frequently of the content features of information. The words *know* or *knowing* to describe the outcome of information were used thirty-three times. Other terms that metaphorically refer to knowledge were used as well—for example, *seeing*, as in "seeing the money going into helping people" or "seeing some of the success stories"; *tell*, as in "tell us this is what these scholarships have done"; and *finding out*, as in "finding out that a new light board was purchased."

The alumni donors also discussed properties of information. Following the model of Senn (1979), donors said they want information that is timely ("I want to know what is going on at the school this year"), frequent ("Quarterly reports would be fine"), complete ("I would like to see that ten people received scholarships"), easily obtained ("I have my hot picks, so I would go to the Web site once a month to see what is going on"), and accurate ("What percentage goes toward the actual goals of the organization?"). Donors pay attention to the form of information they receive ("Whenever I get a response after a donation, I tend to look at the signature and ink").

A final characteristic of properties of information that appeared to be important to donors in the focus groups is the degree of relevance, or irrelevance, of information they receive. Information appears to be relevant when it meets cognitive needs and also emotional needs. Twenty-three times, donors used the word *feel* or *feeling* in their conversation about information. Information about uses of their gifts, or that a dean knew a donor personally, or that students no longer have to wait in long lines for registration makes donors feel good. They used terms like *joy* and *good feeling*, or said, "It was wonderful," to describe their reaction to certain kinds of information. Among the specific good feelings they obtain from information are a sense of being appreciated, recognized, and needed and feelings of pride. Perhaps the most intriguing feeling that alumni donors expressed was one of connectedness to the institution that information helps create. Alumni used the term *connect* or *connectedness* ten times, as in statements like these:

I don't feel connected when I just get a solicitation in the mail.

Over time I have some organizations that I feel a connectedness to. To me, in order to get more alumni to give, you have to improve that connection or their sense of connection to this organization. Until you do that, I don't care what the bottom line is; it is not going to affect them in terms of giving.

In addition to helping identify the content and property information needs of donors, analysis of the focus groups generated specific categories of information need that were used to create a donor questionnaire. Before moving to the category list, however, participants' comments about two categories in particular, thank-you letters and feedback on the uses of their gifts, were especially informative and warrant a more detailed summary.

Donors value the personalization of thank-you letters. Some alumni check out the signature to be sure it is not printed; others recall vividly receiving a handwritten message. Although institutional representatives' thank-you notes are important to most donors, some are well aware of the computerization of such letters and have become jaded to their impact. One participant pointed out that she receives seemingly personalized letters from the president of the United States, so a letter from a university president that is processed by a computer is no longer so impressive. Notes from those who are directly affected by a donor's gift are especially meaningful. Thank-you notes that also ask the donor's advice and counsel are welcomed, and notes that include a mild, but not overt, request for continuing future support are acceptable. Badgering for gifts or asking for gifts on the heels of one gift is resented.

After a gift has been received and acknowledged, donors say they want to learn about the impact of their giving. They want to experience "the joy of knowing you're helping someone." They experience this feeling when they see the results of their giving. Sometimes this "seeing" is direct, as in the case of a parent's gift of clothing to a child in day care whom she later sees wearing the clothing, or a donor coming to campus to meet students who benefit from her gift. Most of the focus group donors, however, want information in the form of reports or other documents to find out about the impact of their giving. Donors want information that will allow them to know they are "helping people lift themselves up to a new level," to see "the transformations that are taking place." In other cases, just knowing exactly what was purchased with one's gift is important. Some donors would like to keep track of students who received scholarships from their gifts even after they graduate. According to one of the focus group participants, having this information helps reaffirm his trust in the institution; he knows that his gifts are being used for good purposes, not for lining the pockets of fundraisers or administrators.

In summary, the focus group participants provided initial answers to the first research question: "What are the information needs of donors?" Donors confirmed that they have information needs, and they spoke of those needs as having both content and property dimensions. Fundraisers need to pay attention to the information they provide to donors and how they provide it. Two categories of information in particular, thank-you letters and feedback on the impact of giving, received in-depth attention by participants, whose comments provide helpful advice to those responsible for stewarding donors and their gifts.

Donor survey

Donors ranked the importance of information on a mailed question-naire (n = 699). The results had very high reliability (alpha = .8948).

Donors were asked if they thought gift receipts were important, and 80 percent said they were. Because the focus group participants mentioned that they used receipts primarily for income tax purposes, it is not surprising that a greater percentage of donors who gave $10,000 or greater wanted receipts (89 percent) than did those who gave under $100 (71 percent), and respondents split evenly on whether they preferred receipts immediately after a gift or at the end of the year.

Surprisingly, fewer donors thought a personal thank-you letter was important (21 percent) than one might have predicted based on focus group comments and the fundraising literature. Nevertheless, the percentage of those who thought a personal thank-you letter was important was considerably higher among $10,000 donors (41.3 percent) than among donors who gave under $100 (13.8 percent). Across all donor groups, donors' first preference was for a thank-you letter from the dean of the college to which they had contributed, and the second preferred choice of top and low-end donors was a letter from the president; a letter from the president was the fourth choice of donors who contributed between $100 and $999. Focus group participants provided a plausible explanation for such an outcome: donors who want thank-you letters want them to be sincere, and they know a letter from a university president for a modest gift is not truly personal.

Donors were asked to rate nine information items on a five-point Likert-type scale ranging from Extremely Important to Not Important. These items reflected categories of content information mentioned by participants in the focus groups. The order of preference for these nine items is as follows, with the percentages indicating responses of Somewhat Important to Extremely Important:

Whether the gift has had a positive impact	82.9 percent
Annual report of area I support	81.9 percent

How much is used for administration	78.7 percent
Annual report of university	73.8 percent
Fundraising needs of the university	70.8 percent
How much was raised from alumni	70.4 percent
Invitations to campus	68.7 percent
Invitation to join the alumni association	57.5 percent
Seeing an honor roll of donors	54.9 percent

Over 80 percent of donors thought that information about the impact of their gift was at least somewhat important. The percentage of donors who thought that each of the information items was at least somewhat important fell as their giving levels declined. However, there was no statistical correlation between giving levels and expressed need for different types of information, a consequence of survey results with very high reliability.

In addition to asking donors about their interest in the content of information, the questionnaire asked about the properties of information, specifically what vehicles donors preferred and how frequently they wanted to receive information. By an overwhelming majority that held true across all donor groups, donors preferred newsletters, from either the areas they supported (68.2 percent) or the university (64.6 percent), over Web sites (26.3 percent), e-mail (24.6 percent), or face-to-face meetings with faculty (15.6 percent) or students (10.7 percent).

As for the frequency of information they receive, donors are in agreement that monthly is too frequent (only 1.7 percent preferred this frequency). They are almost evenly split in their preference for quarterly, semiannual, or annual information.

Support for the meaningful action theory

The findings of this study provide preliminary support for the assumption of a meaningful action theory of giving—that donors have a need for meaning—and specifically for Baumeister's (1991) model that there are four needs for meaning: purpose, value, efficacy, and self-worth.

Donors' need for purpose is shown in their top ranking of the information category of "whether my gift has had a positive impact." In the focus groups, donors stressed the importance of having direct knowledge—of seeing, being told, and finding out—of the impact of their giving. Donors also wanted to be sure to achieve a purpose of taking advantage of tax benefits, so they overwhelmingly agreed that getting a receipt was important.

Donors wanted their values confirmed and clarified through the information they received. In favoring information that verified that they achieved the purpose of helping others through their giving, donors were also expressing a desire to have their goodwill validated. In placing information about how much of gifts is used for administration high on their list, donors were placing a high value on integrity. Loyalty is a value that alumni donors in particular sought to have confirmed through the direct knowledge university officials had of them, and a preference in most cases for thank-you letters from their deans or department heads, who were more likely to know them as alumni.

The search for efficacy—having control over the outcome of their giving—was expressed in the preferences that donors had for the properties of information. Information that comes in a timely way, is frequent (although a third of donors expressed satisfaction with just annual information), is complete, and is easily obtained has the effect of reducing uncertainty in how funds are being used. It is well known that organizations use information to reduce uncertainty so their employees have better control over the outcome of their efforts (Goldhaber, 1986). Information appears to have the same effect on donors: by reducing uncertainty, information increases their sense of efficacy.

Feeling a connection with the university was a major theme that donors in the focus groups expressed, and this sense of connection helps them feel that they are a part of the university, of being a partner through their philanthropy. The need to confirm connection is another way that donors fulfill their need for efficacy.

Finally, donors sought information that satisfied their need for self-worth. The personal thank-you letters that donors spoke so eloquently about in the focus groups were deemed important by a smaller-than-expected number of donors who responded to the survey. This apparent contradiction is understandable, however, when seen in the light of a need for self-worth. In the focus groups, participants emphasized that thank-you letters need to be genuine if they are to be believed and if they are to satisfy one's self-worth. Survey respondents did not have the opportunity to clarify that important quality. They are likely to have responded as they did based on a doubt about the genuineness of such letters, a genuineness that focus group respondents could clarify. In fact, a thank-you letter produced by a computer can diminish one's self-worth and so is likely to be seen as not very important at all. Self-worth comes from the satisfaction of knowing one's gift has had an impact rather than seeing one's name on a list of other donors. Seeing their names listed in honor rolls was the least important kind of information for alumni donors.

Other evidence of meaningful action

The information-needs research reported here is not the only evidence we have of the role that meaning plays in giving. The significant study of donors reported by Prince and File (1994) is an important contribution to our deeper understanding of the role of meaning in giving. Although the authors describe the seven profiles of donor types that emerged from their study as examples of what "motivates" donors, each of their profiles exhibits the four needs for meaning that Baumeister (1991) identified—purpose, values, efficacy, and self-worth:

• *The communitarian.* These donors, mostly businesspeople, are heavily committed to their communities (*purpose*), and they feel a strong desire to repay their communities for the advantages that they have received from the community (*values*). They select local causes rather than national ones (*efficacy*), and they realize that their business status in the community benefits from their involvement in philanthropy (*self-worth*).

• *The devout.* These donors believe it is God's will for them to help others (*purpose*), and they give out of a sense of moral obligation (*values*). More than other types of donors, devouts want the organizations to which they contribute to honor the same values they have (*efficacy*), and they expect the organizations they support to provide them with personal attention and care (*self-worth*).

• *The investor.* Investors give with one eye on the nonprofits they support and the other eye on the maximum utilization of their assets, including tax considerations (*purpose*). These donors feel they are investing in organizations that will use their money wisely (*efficacy*). They believe that nonprofits are superior to government in dealing with social problems (*values*). Because investors have great respect for money and often give sizable amounts, they expect a level of private attention and public recognition that is appropriate for their actions (*self-worth*).

• *The socialite.* Socialites are drawn to the social circle that surrounds nonprofits, and they relish creating enjoyable ways for themselves and others to give (*purpose*). Although socialites are aware of criticisms regarding their method of giving, they give because they believe in what they are doing, not out of any sense of obligation (*values*). Because they have a highly developed social network in their communities, they are convinced that local nonprofits can do a better job of dealing with their community's needs than can the government (*efficacy*). Of course, socialites want attention, but they also want to know that their voices are being heard (*self-worth*).

• *The altruist.* Altruists give in order to grow spiritually (*purpose*), and they believe that giving is a moral imperative (*values*). They evaluate nonprofits based on the people who run them and then feel confident that those people will use their gifts wisely (*efficacy*). Altruists want to be recognized by the organizations they support as the selfless individuals they are; they do not want to be treated like other major donors (*self-worth*).

• *The repayer.* Because they have benefited from the institutions they support, repayers, including alumni, satisfy their feelings of gratitude through giving (*purpose*). Repayers are unique among the seven categories of donors in believing that the wealthy have a special responsibility to give, and they rate their commitment far above any motivations to give (*values*). Because they have been on the receiving end of the services they support, repayers feel a personal sense of the good results that will follow from their giving (*efficacy*). They are less interested than other donor types in individual attention and public recognition, but they do want the organizations they support to appreciate and validate their unique reasons for giving (*self-worth*). The information-needs research reported here confirms Prince and File's findings (1994).

• *The dynast.* Dynasts give to fulfill family traditions and obligations and because giving is part of their self-concept (*purpose*). They also believe that philanthropy is everyone's responsibility, regardless of their wealth (*values*). Dynasts carefully select the nonprofits they support, often employing professional advisers to assist them, because they want to give to nonprofits that make a real difference (*efficacy*). Dynasts expect to build professional and interpersonal relationships with the key individuals in the organizations they support, so that their unique role in philanthropy is understood and appreciated (*self-worth*).

Conclusion

The motivated behavior paradigm dominates the beliefs, values, and techniques of fundraising. This paradigm sees donors motivated to give because of the influence of external triggers. Meaningfulness is much more of the story of why donors give. The information needs that they express provide a preliminary validation of their search for meaning. More needs to be done to explore this concept. First, we need a research program to confirm the elements of a need for meaning in giving. Baumeister's model (1991) is a good place to start, but there may be other approaches as well. Perhaps giving can be understood as a personal project, and research using the Personal Projects Analysis instrument could help us determine the elements of meaning associated with giving (Little, 1998). Meaning in life is often expressed in the form of a story (Bruner, 1990), and narrative analysis might uncover insights into the meaning of giving for donors (Fisher, 1989; Sommer and Baumeister, 1998). Finally, because meaning is socially and culturally influenced (Berger and Luckmann, 1966), research into how donors and institutions construct the meaning of giving could be pursued.

The most important impact that even this early description of meaningful action can have on fundraisers is to change perceptions of donors. Just as Theory Y managers see their employees differently than Theory X managers do (McGregor, 1960), we will see donors differently through the lens of meaningful action theory than we do through the lens of motivated behavior theory. In evaluating the relevance and power of a meaningful action paradigm, we should ask the pragmatic questions, "What would it be like to believe that?" or "What would I be committing myself to if I believed that?" (Bruner, 1990, p. 26).

What it would be like to believe that donors become donors because doing so gives their life meaning, or is meaningful, is that as fundraisers, we would interact with donors on a more frequent and genuine basis. It would mean being sure to discover and meet the information needs of donors as they define those needs. It would mean giving donors opportunities to tell the stories of what it means to them to be donors and of finding ways to infuse those stories into the culture of giving. Most important, a meaningful action theory of giving would remind us that giving needs to be enjoyable, the experience needs to be reenergized on a regular basis, and the job of fundraising is not really about asking, though asking must be done, but about bringing a new joy to the lives of donors by helping them meet their innate needs for purpose, value, efficacy, and self-worth.

References

Barnes, R. C. "Foreword." P.T.P. Wong and P. S. Fry (eds.), *The Human Quest for Meaning: A Handbook of Psychological Research and Clinical Applications*. Hillside, N.J.: Erlbaum, 1998.

Baumeister, R. F. *The Meaning of Life*. New York: Guilford, 1991.

Berger, P. L., and Luckmann, T. *The Social Construction of Meaning: A Treatise in the Sociology of Meaning*. New York: Anchor Books, 1966.

Bruner, J. *Acts of Meaning*. Cambridge, Mass.: Harvard University Press, 1990.

Campbell, C. *The Myth of Social Action*. Cambridge, England: Cambridge University Press, 1996.

Cialdini, R. B. *Influence: The New Psychology and Modern Persuasion*. New York: Quill, 1984.

Dervin, B. "Information as a User Construct: The Relevance of Perceived Information Needs to Synthesis and Interpretation." In S. A. Ward and L. J. Reed (eds.), *Knowledge Structure and Use: Implications for Synthesis and Interpretation*. Philadelphia: Temple University Press, 1983.

Fisher, W. R. *Human Communication as Narration: Toward a Philosophy of Reason, Value, and Action*. Columbia: University of South Carolina Press, 1989.

Frankl, V. E. *Man's Search for Meaning*. (Rev. ed.) New York: Washington Square Press, 1984.

Goldhaber, G. M. *Organizational Communication*. (4th ed.) Dubuque, Iowa: W. C. Brown, 1986.

Herzberg, F. "One More Time: How Do You Motivate Employees?" *Harvard Business Review*, 1987, *65*, 109–120.

Infante, D. A., Rancer, A. S., and Womack, D. F. *Building Communication Theory*. (2nd ed.) Prospect Heights, Ill.: Waveland Press, 1993.

Kelly, K. S. "From Motivation to Mutual Understanding: Shifting the Domain of Donor Research." In D. F. Burlingame (ed.), *Critical Issues in Fundraising*. New York: Wiley, 1997.

Kuhn, T. S. *The Structure of Scientific Revolutions*. (2nd ed.) Chicago: University of Chicago, 1970.

Little, B. R. "Personal Project Pursuit: Dimensions and Dynamics of Personal Meaning." In P.T.P. Wong and P. S. Fry (eds.), *The Human Quest for Meaning: A Handbook of Psychological Research and Clinical Applications*. Hillside, N.J.: Erlbaum, 1998.

McGregor, D. *The Human Side of Enterprise*. New York: McGraw-Hill, 1960.

Means, D. R. "Charting Futures for Sociology: Culture and Meaning, the Social Construction of Meaning." *Contemporary Sociology*, 2000, *29*, 577–584.

Mutz, J., and Murray, K. *Fundraising for Dummies*. Chicago: IDG Books, 2000.

Myers, D. G. "The Importance of Stewardship." In M. K. Murphy (ed.), *Building Bridges: Fundraising for Deans, Faculty, and Development Officers*. Washington, D.C.: Council for Advancement and Support of Education, 1992.

Ostrower, F. *Why the Wealthy Give: The Culture of Elite Philanthropy*. Princeton, N.J.: Princeton University Press, 1995.

Prince, R. A., and File, K. M. *The Seven Faces of Philanthropy: A New Approach to Cultivating Major Donors.* San Francisco: Jossey-Bass, 1994.

The Random House Dictionary of the English Language. New York: Random House, 1979.

Ritzenhein, D. N. "A Qualitative and Quantitative Analysis of the Information Needs of Alumni Donors to Wayne State University." Unpublished doctoral dissertation, Wayne State University, 1999.

Schneiter, P. H. *The Art of Asking: How to Solicit Philanthropic Gifts.* (2nd ed.) Ambler, Pa.: Fund-Raising Institute, 1985.

Senn, J. *Information Systems in Management.* Belmont, Calif.: Wadsworth, 1979.

Seymour, H. J. *Designs for Fund-Raising.* (2nd ed.) Ambler, Pa.: Fund-Raising Institute, 1988.

Sommer, K. L., and Baumeister, R. F. "The Construction of Meaning from Life Events: Empirical Studies of Personal Narratives." In P.T.P. Wong and P. S. Fry (eds.), *The Human Quest for Meaning: A Handbook of Psychological Research and Clinical Applications.* Hillside, N.J.: Erlbaum, 1998.

Watzlawick, P., Beavin, J. H., and Jackson, D. D. *Pragmatics of Human Communication: A Study of Interactional Patterns, Pathologies, and Paradoxes.* New York: Norton, 1967.

Wong, P.T.P., and Fry, P. S. "Introduction." In P.T.P. Wong and P. S. Fry (eds.), *The Human Quest for Meaning: A Handbook of Psychological Research and Clinical Applications.* Hillside, N.J.: Erlbaum, 1998.

DONALD N. RITZENHEIN *is assistant vice president for annual giving and development services at Wayne State University, Detroit, Michigan.*

*To engage donors of color, nonprofit organizations
must understand the importance and interconnectedness of morality, market, and mission.*

5

The new rules for engaging donors of color: Giving in the twenty-first century

Emmett D. Carson

MY TASK in this chapter is to write about "emerging philanthropy
from minority populations" and the impact that their philanthropy
is having on the nonprofit sector. I also want to share some observations about the so-called new donor. It is important to state at
the outset that donors of color are not new donors. Quite the con-
trary; many racial and ethnic groups have charitable giving traditions that predate the founding of the United States.

Let me also begin by confessing a bias. I don't know anything
more, and hopefully nothing less, than all of the other people who
are speculating about the interests, values, and beliefs of new
donors. At this early stage of the golden age of philanthropy, anyone who presumes to tell anybody how the new donors will affect
either philanthropy or the nonprofit sector is really just guessing.
In a wonderful article in *Business 2.0*, Peter Drucker states that an

Note: This chapter was adapted from a keynote address presented at Donor Dynamics
Beyond the Comfort Zone, Indiana University Center on Philanthropy Thirteenth
Annual Symposium, Aug. 25, 2000.

NEW DIRECTIONS FOR PHILANTHROPIC FUNDRAISING, NO. 29, FALL 2000 © JOHN WILEY & SONS, INC.

invention is probably used the way the inventor originally intended less than 10–15 percent of the time (Daly, 2000). He goes on to say that it is usually someone else from a different field who envisions how the invention can be used to solve a different problem and who makes millions bringing the new idea to market. My comments are based on how I see the world today. I reserve the right to be influenced by new developments that may lead me to think differently in the future based on new information. It is in this spirit that I address four topics.

First, I examine why there is such a growing interest by nonprofit organizations in donors of color. Second, there is a comment on how the not-so-old rules of engagement continue to hamper efforts to successfully solicit donors of color. Third, I describe the new rules of engagement for interacting with donors of color and how these new rules can help nonprofit organizations raise funds and other support from donors of color. And fourth, I offer some observations to those who appear to be overly enamored with the idea of the new donor.

Why the interest in donors of color?

Why does everyone suddenly care about donors of color? I have been talking about donors of color and the impact that they will have on the nonprofit sector for over fifteen years, and suddenly everybody is interested. The presidential nominating conventions of the two major political parties in 2000 were reaching out to people of color, each saying, "I can outdo you on diversity!" What has happened? What has changed? The answer is that the United States is finally coming to the collective recognition that the citizen of today and tomorrow is less likely to be a white male. This understanding is also being applied to the new voter, the new worker, and the "new" donor. As this recognition takes place, organizations and institutions are having to shift and expand their attention from their traditional constituencies (established through past history, cultural affinity, and social stereotypes) to respond to new groups of people.

Smart executives in business, government, and the nonprofit sectors are trying to position themselves in the eyes of everyday people to say, "We didn't always do the right thing in the past in terms of our relationships with people of color, but we're doing the right things now." I sincerely applaud companies like Aetna for stepping up and acknowledging their historical involvement in the slave trade (Robertson and Kerber, 2000). Aetna has acted with integrity and honesty. The question is how organizations will acknowledge past acts with regard to people of color. Will it be in the same way that George W. Bush, as the Republican presidential nominee, tried to say that the Republican party was trying to get right with people of color? Whether you think his message was sincere, he was saying that Republicans have not always reached out to communities of color but from that moment on were going to change. By contrast, Al Gore, the Democratic presidential nominee, argued that his party's actions and its words had demonstrated that its members value the needs, interests, and involvement of people of color.

Nonprofit organizations increasingly are going to have to ask whether there are things in their history that need to be acknowledged. As the donor base becomes more diverse, as people look different, as people of color bring different views and values to their pursuits, nonprofit organizations will need to ask themselves, "How have we acted over the course of our organization's history?" The good news is that an organization just started last month does not have much of a history. That is an advantage, because it has not had time to do anything wrong. But there are a lot of people in the community who might say that a particular institution that is, say, eighty years old was not there for them when some event happened. This organization may need to acknowledge this publicly in order for all involved to start with a clean slate.

Considerations of diversity are complicated by the fact that we live in a global marketplace. Almost anything can be produced anywhere, and technology allows information and money to be transferred almost instantaneously. The United States must now see itself as part of a larger world economy. Though we are becoming very diverse within the United States, the rest of the world is even more diverse. A national or international charity may not only need to reexamine its relationships with people of color within the United States; it may also need to examine its history with people from around the world. How will citizens from countries in Asia, Africa, or South America feel about how their country is depicted in a particular museum collection? How are they presented? How do exhibits present the key events of their history? Does each group feel affirmed as a culture? Do they feel that they are presented in a negative light? Is the collection viewed as having been legitimately obtained, or will residents of the country in question perceive that the collection was stolen?

I once had the opportunity to visit Nigeria. I collect African art, so I was pleased to visit the major museum. But I was shocked to see that the museum largely consisted of photographs of artifacts that are on display at the British Museum. Underneath the photographs, caption after caption read: "Stolen property held at the British Museum." Nonprofit organizations will have to grapple with these kinds of issues as they fully accept the implications of living in the global world.

The old rules for engaging donors of color

What are the old rules for engaging donors of color that make it difficult for nonprofit organizations to solicit funds and support from these communities? The single biggest old rule that gets in the way of developing healthy relationships with donors of color is perception. We act based on how we think about things. When an organization starts off with a perception that people of color have no giving traditions—even subtly, as in my assignment to write about the "emerging" philanthropy of donors of color—it has already made a terrible mistake.

African Americans have a two-hundred-year tradition of giving and volunteering that can be directly traced back to traditions of giving and volunteering in Africa. Because we see it and recognize it today, we refer to it as emerging. Confucianism talks about charitable giving. This religion is older than our country. And yet we go to an Asian person who practices the tenets of Confucianism and say that his or her philanthropy is emerging. Every racial and ethnic group, as well as every major religion, has long and established traditions of giving and volunteering (Carson, 1995). The problem is our perceptions. We do not mean to be off-putting to people of color or to have a bias. But we do not question the assumptions that we use when we interact with people. As a result, we say things in our initial conversations that can be insulting to the very people we want to embrace (Carson, 1994).

Another popular assumption is that people of color do not have any money. Who would not want to have Oprah Winfrey as a major donor? Michael Jordan? Michael Jackson? The incoming chief executive officer of American Express, Kenneth Chenault? Yet our stereotypes that people of color are more likely to be recipients rather than givers of philanthropy prevent us from effectively communicating.

Over the years, I have had the opportunity to talk to numerous development officers who have said that they research every aspect of a potential donor's life before they meet with the person. After numerous overtures, the development officer finally gets a meeting that lasts thirty minutes. The potential donor barely grunts over the lunch, and the development officer goes back to the office and writes a report that says, "I think we're making progress." This example is consistent with what I have heard over and over: that fund development is a cultivation process.

Now send the same development officer out to meet with a potential donor of color. The development officer writes a brief letter that says he or she would like to meet the potential donor to talk about the work of the nonprofit organization. The development officer does little to no background research on the donor or her interests—in part, because the development officer has no networks on the board or in the community who have social links to the potential donor. The potential donor agrees to an initial meeting, and before dessert is served, the development officer asks, "Will you contribute $25,000 to our organization?" The donor of color says, "I've got to think about this a bit." The development officer goes back to the office and reports, "See, people of color don't give." The perception is different; the expectations are different.

Moreover, people of color know when they have been treated poorly. They understand when someone approaches them who does not take the time to get to know them and yet somehow expects them to be thrilled at the opportunity to give $25,000. What is more surprising is how, given this behavior, a development officer could call into question the personal philanthropy of the potential donor of color or that of his or her entire racial or ethnic community. Notwithstanding these experiences, many fund development officers continue to have different perceptions and expectations of donors of color. Donors of color do give. The challenge is for nonprofit organizations to determine correctly why these donors are not giving to their organizations.

The last old rule that gets in the way of engaging donors of color is language. The notion of who is in the minority and who represents the majority in terms of race and ethnicity has changed. We are going to have an increasingly tough time talking about who is in the majority. If you go to Los Angeles, Chicago, or Atlanta, the notion of who is in the majority is different and changing. The terms *minority* and *majority* refer to an old language that says a lot about whether a nonprofit organization has entered the twenty-first century or remains stuck in the twentieth century.

The new rules for engaging donors of color

To engage donors of color, nonprofit organizations must understand the importance and interconnectedness of morality, market, and mission. Nonprofit organizations can no longer represent themselves as one thing to one donor and something entirely different to another donor. The free flow of information today does not allow nonprofit organizations to do that anymore. No organization can represent itself with five different images on its Web site.

It has to be one thing to all people. Too many of us approach donors by saying, "What are you interested in?" and responding, "We can do that."

The new donor dynamics require that each nonprofit organization know its mission. It may thrive or die, but it will do that based on what its mission is. People may or may not agree with a particular organization, but if it is a direct service provider, it cannot suddenly become something else. This approach may mean taking some public stances. It may require that the organization adhere to its strategic directions rather than trying to be all things to all people.

An important worldview held by many new donors, especially from the technology sector, is that they are far more comfortable with the implications of a multicultural society than older donors and most nonprofit organizations are. It appears that the new donors from high-tech industries have a low tolerance for racial bias and age discrimination. People are valued based on their contributions, not their personal characteristics. This is a welcome outlook that may require significant changes by nonprofit organizations and their staffs as they interact with donors who hold these perspectives.

The new rules of engagement make identifying potential donors more difficult. For example, many corporate offices around the country have converted to business casual dress. The problem is that you no longer know to whom you might be talking because of the way the person is dressed. In our mind's eye, we have an image of the donor. Because perceptions can get in the way, I need to state the obvious: People of color use the Internet. People of color are part of the new high-tech wealth. People of color are younger donors. People of color are part of all the things we talk about related to the new donor, and yet I doubt that they are images that come to mind when we talk about the new donor. The new reality is forcing us to be more honest in spending time with all people, regardless of who walks in the door, because you do not know who they are or for whom they might be a representative. This is a good development for the nonprofit sector, because too often we have ignored people we should have listened to who could make contributions to the work of the organization.

Some of the most consistent donors are people who start off with small gifts to see how they are treated and to determine the value of the organization's work. These donors want to get to know and understand what a particular organization is about. When these donors arrive in their everyday casual dress, we are going to have to treat each of them with respect and enthusiasm—notwithstanding perceptions about race, ethnicity, class, or gender.

The authors of *The Millionaire Next Door* (Stanley and Danko, 1996) state that the new millionaire buys a used car and stays in the same older home he or she has always lived in. This person does not have many of the ostentatious symbols of wealth that allow us to say, "Oh, you might have something, and therefore I need to pay attention to you." These millionaires are not on anyone's list, and they do not stand out in ways that make them easy to identify as being wealthy.

Finally, it is clear that donors put an increasing emphasis on results (Carson, 2000; "Grantmakers in Search of a Holy Grail," 2000). In this aspect, donors of color mirror other donors. Nonprofit organizations are going to have to address the issue of evaluation more forthrightly than they have and recognize cultural sensitivities and their own perceptions in explaining why something does or does not work. They must find better ways to explain, without being defensive, that in some areas they can show amazing, concrete results and for others they cannot. In this regard, they are like medical doctors who have excellent proven treatments for some maladies and only experimental treatments for others.

The area of education is a good example. Over seventy languages are spoken in the Minneapolis and St. Paul public schools. For people who question why urban education is so difficult to reform, I encourage them to spend a day learning why it is so difficult for Johnny to learn to read. It is not because of all those "other" children in the schools; instead, it is a greater challenge for teachers to educate a heterogeneous class than a homogeneous one. I encourage these donors to share with foundation staff what they think educators have missed. Most often, these donors move from unrealistic expectations about results to having an intricate and nuanced understanding of the complexity of urban education and how progress can be made by all of the children and how quickly. Such donor education is more time-consuming, but it is preferable to the alternative of nonprofit organizations that make unrealistic promises to solve problems for which no successful solutions have been developed or the equally troubling outcome of inappropriately suggesting that the lack of results has to do with the race or ethnicity of the people involved in the program.

Reflections on the new donor

For all of the discussion about the new donor, there is little common agreement on who we are really talking about. Are we talking about the entrepreneur who started her business and sold it for a large profit? Are we talking about the young corporate executive with stock options who now has an opportunity to cash out? Are we talking about the elderly person who has worked all of his life for a single company and has accumulated large cash balances in his 401(k)? Are we talking about the dot-com millionaire? There are too many things that are being lumped into the new donor–new wealth category. It is essential that we clarify what specific target group is under discussion so that the generalizations that are made are accurate.

Maturity

I do not think the way I thought when I was twenty or thirty years old. Most of us evolve, change, and mature. Underlying much of the discussion about younger donors is the basic assumption that they will continue to hold the same views and disperse their charitable assets in the same ways as they get older. There is no reason to believe that as younger donors age and mature, they will not act and behave in the same ways that their mothers and fathers do today. If nonprofit organizations disproportionately shift their focus to respond to younger donors, they may find themselves out of sync as these donors mature through the life cycle, and they may unnecessarily alienate current older donors. This is not to suggest that nonprofit organizations should not be responsive to the temperaments and perspectives of younger donors, but rather to be mindful that as this target demographic group ages, they may not want the same things as they get older.

Keeping it is different from making it

I differ with those who suggest that someone who is wealthy today will continue to be wealthy several years from now. I am an economist by training, and I understand that the market works in cycles. Economic depressions can hit for prolonged periods of time, but even when they do not, individuals can become involved in unsuccessful business ventures. The notion of once wealthy, always wealthy is false. Amazon.com has yet to make a profit despite millions upon millions in investments. The nightly news is filled with stories of formerly wealthy dot-com millionaires whose paper profits have evaporated, seemingly overnight (Pulliam, 2000).

Wealth transfer versus new wealth

I continue to think that the immediate opportunity in this golden age of philanthropy will be the wealth transfer of senior citizens, not the new wealth of younger donors. I understand older donors. I understand the life experiences that have helped to shape their reality. And I know that time is limited if they are going to be encouraged to engage in philanthropy during their lifetimes and beyond through estate planning. Compare this opportunity with that represented by the young entrepreneurs, whom I do not quite understand and, whom, despite all the hype, I cannot seem to locate. The reality is that younger donors are going to age, and those who are able to keep what they make will be accessible later. This is not to say that younger donors should be ignored, but rather they should not become the exclusive focus of fund development efforts at the expense of efforts to reach older donors.

About religion

A lot has been said about the spiritual and religious dimension in promoting philanthropy. We would all do well to remember that there are a lot of people who are not Judeo-Christian. As our nation continues to diversify, so will the range of religious beliefs. When we start assuming that a specific set of religious beliefs, such as Christianity, is useful in motivating people to engage in philanthropy, we fall into the trap of letting our perceptions mislead us. If you are talking to someone who is Muslim, you need to understand the implications of the religious or spiritual example that you want to use for the intent of motivating that person to be more charitable. This is probably not accomplished with an example from the Bible. Once we start to understand the different cultures, we will understand and appreciate that our meaning and intentions can be interpreted very differently from our intentions.

The estate tax

There is a great deal of national discussion about the fairness of estate tax. One aspect of this issue that has not received much attention is that many of us in the nonprofit sector firmly believe that the repeal of the estate tax will have disastrous negative consequences on the growth and sustainability of the nonprofit sector. One reason this has not received attention is that nonprofit organizations are reluctant to speak out for fear that our wealthy donors (who may benefit from the estate tax repeal) will take offense. Our sector's lack of a public voice on this issue is disheartening. Universities, hospitals, museums, and community foundations, as well as the larger membership associations of these groups, are all complicit in their collective silence. When I talk with people who are very wealthy, many of them have already reached the point where they think they have given enough to their children. Their question is, "What should I do with the rest?" It is a strong incentive to say to them to give it to charity or give it to the government. In nearly every case, donors would rather direct the money to charity than give it to the government. Without this incentive, nonprofit organizations and the causes that they support are likely to find it far more difficult to raise charitable resources.

Conclusion

The conventional wisdom is that the past is often a prelude to the future. If this is true as it relates to the golden age of philanthropy, we are likely to squander the enormous opportunities presented by donors of color, the wealth transfer of seniors, and the new wealth being created by the high-tech industry. Organized philanthropy and the nonprofit sector have had difficulty adjusting to the realities of the new multicultural society and global marketplace. Only by changing our collective perceptions of who gives and how we approach them—establishing new rules of engagement—can we hope and expect to reach the promise and potential of the golden era of philanthropy. My hope is that the promise and potential of this new era spur us to adopt new rules for engaging both donors of color and the different types of new donors.

References

Carson, E. D. "Community Foundations, Racial Diversity, and Institutional Change." In R. C. Hedgepeth (ed.), *Nonprofit Organizational Culture: What Fundraisers Need to Know*. New Directions for Philanthropic Fundraising, no. 5. San Francisco: Jossey-Bass, 1994.

Carson, E. D. "The Colors of Money: Charitable Giving Among Racial and Ethnic Minorities." *Colors*, May–June 1995, p. 14.

Carson, E. D. "On Foundations and Outcome Evaluation." *Nonprofit and Voluntary Sector Quarterly*, 2000, *29*, 479–481.

Daly, J. "Sage Advice." *Business 2.0*, Aug. 22, 2000, pp. 136–144.

"Grantmakers in Search of a Holy Grail: A Heretic's Reflections on Neighborhood Assets, Outcomes Evaluation and Venture Capital Investing." *Foundation News and Commentary*, 2000, *41*, 24–26.

Pulliam, S. "What Goes Up: For Some Executives the Internet Dream Has a Deep Downside." *Wall Street Journal*, Oct. 20, 2000, pp. A1–A6.

Robertson, T., and Kerber, R. "Slave Trade History Gets a Fresh Look." *Star Tribune* (Minneapolis, Minn.), Aug. 18, 2000, p. 9E.

Stanley, T. J., and Danko, W. D. *The Millionaire Next Door: The Surprising Secrets of America's Wealthy*. Marietta, Ga.: Longstreet Press, 1996.

EMMETT D. CARSON *is president and CEO of the Minneapolis Foundation.*

Donors face complex challenges in bridging the gap between their private selves and the public interest, and they may never be able to do so unless they are motivated, educated, nudged, and supported in the process.

6

The public and private persona of philanthropy: The donor challenge

H. Peter Karoff

PRIVATE ACTION in a public space. Hmm, what a curious idea!

That, of course, is what philanthropy is. It starts with what is most personal and most private—our values and passions—and moves to a transaction, of money or time or both, that is enacted in public. This is so regardless of recognition. The source of the gift may be anonymous, but it displays itself in full view of some larger audience. Indeed, the charitable gift is made within the construct of tax benefits permitted only because the act is presumed to provide a public good. Philanthropy straddles two domains, the self (individual, institutional, or corporate) and the public arena, however defined.

I like the notion of philanthropy as a bridge and the way that revelation is possible when, with "our works," we cross it and in the process create a new persona that is neither private nor public but something that transcends both.

For the past eleven years, my organization, The Philanthropic Initiative (TPI), has been working to develop models and services

NEW DIRECTIONS FOR PHILANTHROPIC FUNDRAISING, NO. 29, FALL 2000 © JOHN WILEY & SONS, INC.

that help donors, individuals, family foundations, corporations, and community foundations become more in touch with their values and more strategic in their giving. We have done so through a variety of mechanisms that include a wide range of educational programs that have reached more than eight thousand wealthy individuals and their advisers, as well as a direct consulting practice that in 2001 will help clients invest more than $80 million in a wide range of issue areas. As a result, we have been on the front lines and have observed how complex it is for donors to bridge the two domains of individual and public interest.

Our work has been a kind of dialogue between individuals and their values, passions, goals, and interests—a dialogue within a family or a board of trustees and foundation staff; a dialogue between a development officer and a potential donor, within a corporation and its multiple stakeholders; and a dialogue between a United Way or a community foundation and its various stakeholders and constituencies. The gift process itself is a form of meeting and dialogue, sometimes weak and formulaic (you send a check to the local land trust and get a form letter back thanking you) and sometimes robust and meaningful (you make a major gift to an organization that allows it to purchase a building that reduces its real estate cost down to almost zero).

None of this is simple. The donor has to make a decision to act for a broader mission, however defined. Some do it naturally, and others never do. Much of our work at TPI has been to move the dialogue from being "sight unseen" to being on the table, where it can be looked at, talked about, and resolved. At this point in our organization's life, we are especially interested in working with clients who are serious, that is, have a real interest in developing a higher order of a public persona.

The majority of donors in the world of philanthropy do not begin with such concerns, not in the sense that most fundraisers might have. Most donors, including the vast majority of the more than fifty thousand private foundations and the several hundred thousand donor-advised funds, operate what might be called checkbook philanthropy. The notion of what might be called citizenship philanthropy, which reflects a broader, more public social agenda, is primarily limited to the realm of the larger established foundations and a relatively small percentage of family and corporate donors.

In my view, turning those ratios around is the central challenge, the make-or-break issue on whether we really have a new golden age of philanthropy.

We have observed in both our practice and in the discussions in many workshops and symposiums that people start at a certain place, and almost always their first instinct is to "pay back" in a predictable manner to those places to which they feel an allegiance—often a college or a university or a hospital. They may then become receptive to something broader or bigger, or both.

In a major TPI report just completed, *What's a Donor to Do? The State of Donor Resources in America Today*, my colleague Ellen Remmer (2000) describes the journey that donors make. The best donors are deeply engaged in and committed to their giving and are always learning about how to make their giving more effective. Most new and emerging donors are not yet there in the journey. In fact, many do not recognize the potential—not to mention what it takes—to get there. And many will never get there unless they are motivated, educated, nudged, and supported in the process.

In an effort to understand better how to reach and support new and emerging donors, we have developed a framework that categorizes donors in three stages based on a continuum of experience and engagement with philanthropy. The categories are a useful way to think about how a new, inexperienced donor evolves into an effective, engaged philanthropist:

Stage 1: Dormant but receptive. This donor is willing to make gifts if asked but is basically passive; philanthropy is not a big part of his or her life. Most new and emerging donors or would-be donors fall into this category.

Stage 2: Engaged; getting organized. This donor is more connected to giving and may have established a management/transactional vehicle, such as a donor-advised fund or even a foundation. Most such donors are not yet thinking strategically, and they are only beginning to be proactive. Although considerably fewer donors are in this stage than in stage 1, this group is growing quickly.

Stage 3: Committed; becoming a learner. Philanthropy has become a major part of this donor's life, and she or he is committed to making a difference. This donor is an active learner, and her or his giving is the closest analogue to professional philanthropy, however defined.

For the purpose of the transition of self to the larger world, the stage 1 donor is still operating as a private persona, and the stage 2 donor is beginning to make the transition from at least a process point of view to a more public persona. The stage 3 donor, because she is a continuous learner, is the recipient of experience and knowledge that reflects the broadest perspective and has achieved the most public persona of all. In TPI's philanthropic curve, an earlier rendition of this kind of progressive journey, the stage 3 donor has reached a kind of nirvana, with values and passions driving a philanthropy that is strategic, innovative, and sensitive to both the private and public nuance.

What is next, perhaps, is to reflect on the primary challenges that donors face in reaching toward the kind of transformation we are describing.

The challenge of values

You are on record as a supporter of low- and moderate-income housing, but all of a sudden there is a project proposed that is literally in your backyard and everyone in the neighborhood, your spouse included, is against it. Do you lend your support?

Your foundation supports health issues and environmental programs, but the foundation's investment portfolio includes tobacco and alcohol companies, as well as some of the worst corporate polluters in the world. Your lawyer keeps talking about the "prudent man rule." Are you willing to "walk the walk"?

The corporation you work for is on record against human rights violations and abusive child labor, but an investigative reporter finds that the conditions in the plants of your subcontractors in China are horrible. There are big financial implications in making changes. What does management do?

At a recent conference on wealth and society sponsored by Citi-Group, we did a workshop on values and used a set of questions to frame the discussion: What are the three most important experiences in your life that formed your values? Who are the people, historical or literary, who most influenced you? What are your values? What are your community values? How does your giving fit with your values?

One of the participants, a former governor, said what we have heard so often before: "My values and my giving do not match!" Isn't that interesting? Without a doubt, it is the reconciliation of values with practice that signals a major crossing of the bridge between the private and the public persona. That means stepping back and taking stock. In our several hundred discussions on values, individual and corporate, the internal, family, or corporate dialogue is almost always revelatory.

The challenge of hubris

"I am going to give $100 million to Madison, Wisconsin, for an arts center, whether the city wants it or not!"

One of our clients has extended an offer to the Abkhaz Republic to create a wireless communication system for the entire country that would bring that very poor and backward region into the twenty-first century. He also has a noble subagenda. He hopes to create a paradigm shift from an economy based on consumption, a society based on selfishness and war, to one of greater focus on spirituality and consciousness. He hopes his act of generosity will be the metaphor to open the minds and hearts of the country's leaders. We are concerned he will be perceived as an unwelcome white knight on a white horse in a brown world.

We met a woman some years ago who wanted to use her foundation to run guns to Guatemala. In her view, supporting revolution and violence in the name of freedom was acceptable. She was not a Guatemalan.

In the early 1960s, I joined a group of well-meaning young activists who had "adopted" a thirty-six-block area of Roxbury, then a predominantly African American neighborhood in Boston. We were going to fix up the housing and, while we were at it, fix up the people who lived there too. None of us lived in Roxbury. We all lived in the suburbs. One evening just before Martin Luther King, Jr., was assassinated, I had the rare experience of having a chair thrown at me by the vice president of the Boston National Association for the Advancement of Colored People. At the time I did not understand. Now I do.

The challenge of donor control and engagement

"I want to control and direct the philanthropic action." At what point is donor direction inappropriate or counterproductive? Money is power, and cash is king, but what qualifies the donor to be the operator?

Several years ago, we were working with a family foundation, and the principal trustee became interested in after-school programs for very poor children. After we had presented the results of our research and recommended that the foundation could fill significant gaps within community-based organizations that work with children, our client told us, "I want to pursue this, but I don't just want to give grants. I want my own program."

Well, what did that mean? Our client was smart but hardly an expert and had no experience or interest whatsoever in running programs. What it meant for us was a careful, and somewhat sensitive, probing and ultimately a suggestion to create a defined, strategic, and innovative portfolio of exemplary programs. The program had a name, a dedicated staff, and was sufficiently "her own program" to be satisfying to our client.

Donors do want their own program, and they want to put their stamp on it. And so they should, but with an eye to windward, so to speak.

There is a real trend toward deeper levels of engagement in concepts like venture philanthropy, which we applaud. Engagement is essential, but I have to admit that during one presentation from an advocate of one version of venture philanthropy, I had the distinct sense that most nonprofits would be better off not taking the money. There are too many hoops to jump through and too much loss of control.

The challenge of fear

"I would like to do some things in Roxbury [substitute Harlem or Watts, for example] but do not know where it is and would be afraid to go there." These words came from a lifelong resident of Boston. There is fear of the unknown, and the media nightly exacerbate the negative stereotypes with which we live.

"No good deed goes unpunished," one of our clients loves to say, quoting the inimitable Clare Booth Luce. What am I getting into when I walk into unfamiliar terrain? Will it come back to me in ways I do not want, such as media attention?

The first rule of philanthropy is to do no harm: "How do I know this decision will not hurt someone?"

I am afraid of failure, of looking ridiculous, of my ideas not being accepted, of being attacked.

The challenge of defining public good

I am someone who believes in the right of a woman to control her own body and, if she deems it necessary, to have an abortion. Or I am someone who is pro-life and believe that it is against God's will to end a pregnancy.

I support charter schools and vouchers for all children in the United States. Or I believe that public schools are an essential part of the United States and that universal vouchers will destroy the system.

I believe in the vision of the free market system and the underlying concepts of the new economy. Or I believe in the vision of the civil society as Senator Bill Bradley has defined it: "The realm of family, friends, neighbors, schools, churches and the values of reciprocity, respect, trust, stability, civic involvement and love" (Yankelovich, 1999).

Which represents the public good, or do they both? Does one's private passion give the right to repress another's private passion? Or are there lines one should not cross? At some point, is it our responsibility to enter into a dialogue with others?

The challenge of a greater good

In the hierarchy of philanthropic good, is the gift to the museum or the university less important than the gift to the homeless shelter? Peter Goldmark, former president of the Rockefeller Foundation, has said that it is no longer enough to do nice things with your philanthropy; it is time to do the important things.

How do you define importance? In the words of Paul Ylvisaker, are you steward, change agent, or venture capitalist?

Is parochialism really supporting the public good? I give only to Jewish issues; or I give only to Catholic issues; or I give only to Christian issues.

When is my gift self-serving? This is an actual quotation: "I bought the land across from my property on the Intercoastal Waterway and gifted it to a land trust. My view is forever clear—and by the way, my property value has increased."

My corporate contributions program is integral to the company and its business mission; the objective is a social and business bottom line. Which counts more: the cause-related marketing program supported by big dollars from the marketing department, or the modest but targeted investment in a new pilot program to help welfare mothers make the transition to work?

Few new donors are taking on the big systemic issues that have been the domain of the large national foundations, like persistent poverty and race relations. Many want to but do not know how or are frustrated by the system. We have a client who said, "I know how to give $100 million to Stanford. I don't know how to give $100 million to the kids in the city, and that is what I would rather do."

How many donors write big checks to big institutions by default rather from conviction?

___

The challenge of transparency, of being a fiduciary

When GuideStar Web site (www.guidestar.org) made available the IRS Form 990s of private foundations, some of the very largest were upset. Many private foundations are concerned about privacy and much prefer to keep their affairs confidential. The law may be clear about these funds' constituting a public trust and the role of the trustees as fiduciaries, but many trustees have only a vague sense of what that is.

New family foundations have a major policy decision to make at the start: to what extent the enterprise is going to be a collective experience versus simply dividing the resources among the participants. To begin the transition from checkbook to citizenship, philanthropy often begins at this point. The challenge with families is to find a community of interest within the collective values and passions of the individuals involved that is truly compelling—more compelling than simply adding to the charitable giving budgets of the individuals. Although this is only a preliminary step, it often leads to a first-ever strategic initiative, one that by process and application can move the participants to thinking more broadly and more publicly about an issue.

___

The challenge of knowledge

I remember the first time we met the trustees of the Melville Charitable Trust, who decided to focus the trust's work on the single issue of homelessness. "But," they said, "all we know is what we read in the *New York Times*. We need to know more." The trustees at that time were in their early sixties, and over a period of a year, we conducted a tutorial that provided the context for the policy decisions that have driven the trust since. Over ten years, the trust has become not only the largest funder focused on homelessness in Connecticut, but wonderfully smart about how it does it.

As our understanding increases, we grow. It broadens us, and our perspective becomes increasingly public. TPI's practice is research based, and we have learned that when our clients have been able to disaggregate these huge terms—*education, environment, health care*—they can begin to make sense out of what to do. When the needs have been analyzed and it becomes clear where the gaps are and where the available resources can actually make a difference, donors rise and meet the opportunity.

One of our recommendations in the *What's a Donor to Do?* report (Remmer, 2000) is to establish much enhanced learning systems for donors, regardless of where they are on their philanthropic journey. In our view, this is a major unrealized opportunity for community foundations, United Ways, and others. It is also an opportunity that could be realized by the growing number of mixed-motive players, charitable gift funds, private banks, and investment firms. The biggest opportunity, however, may lie with nonprofit organizations that have the intellectual substance about issues and programs that donors want. We think fundraising that provides donors with information that goes beyond the typical case statement into a true learning experience is where the field is going. And lest this sound excessively supply side or paternalistic, donors have consistently told us that they would welcome such knowledge.

We are increasingly excited about the role that corporations can play as knowledge providers and as brokers to society. In particular, the response within the corporate sector to innovative programs designed to engage employees in giving and volunteering is very encouraging. Our experience at America Online in the design of the Giving Tree Service, a company-wide philanthropic advisory service, is one example. The success of Putnam Investments in motivating senior executives to form a giving circle is another.

The challenge of ambition

We have one client who has established a large new foundation dedicated to the critical issue of tolerance. He is motivated by the rise of totalitarian movements in Europe as well as the words of Rodney King: "Why can't we get along?"

An extraordinary initiative by the Joseph Family Foundation in East Los Angeles is under way. The objective is to transform a neighborhood. Over several years, the foundation has built a multifaceted relationship with that community. It has gone so well that the Joseph family decided to invest the entire corpus of the foundation, some $40 million, in a community-controlled community development corporation that will sponsor housing and economic development, including a much-needed supermarket.

One of the amazing philanthropic stories is the voyage of Ray Chambers, who has almost singlehandedly transformed the city of Newark, New Jersey, and the children who live there. Over a decade, Chambers has invested more than $50 million in a wide range of youth-related programs, provided the lead in the building of the remarkable $300 million New Jersey Performing Arts Center, syndicated the purchase of the New Jersey Nets by a charitable trust with the proviso that the team move from the nearby Meadowlands into Newark, and through his organization, One-to-One, become the model for the Colin Powell–led America's Promise. Chambers is a quiet man who made every mistake in the book and kept coming back for more, until he got it right.

Sometimes there is not enough ambition—no fire in the belly. Donors have not been sufficiently engaged or excited to do more than the obvious—the donor for whom finding a passion remains elusive.

Sometimes there is the almost embarrassing marginalization of philanthropy, say, a $5 million foundation in a family worth a billion dollars or more.

It would be incorrect to imply that philanthropic ambition relates to size. Small gifts can and do make a difference. Ambition has more to do with one's state of mind than one's pocketbook. If there is any doubt on this point, take a look at Paul Ylvisaker's wonderful little book on great small grants (1989).

The challenge of process

We think there is a direct link between good process and many of the ideas in the preceding sections. Process determines what the nature of the relationship is between a donor and a donee. Is it fair, open, a two-way learning experience, collegial, and rigorous? Is the dialogue one that builds the capacity of organizations and the people who run them? Is the process one that is fun, that engages both parties, that makes you want to come back for more? Examples are a request for proposals that is carefully drawn to encourage creativity and innovation, or an evaluation process designed to help the donee do a better job, that includes technical assistance, that understands that convening is a wonderfully public way for all the interested parties to learn from one another.

The major public intermediaries, including community foundations and United Ways, are at the heart of practicing and teaching good process. They are on the front line to the largest number of donors and represent a major bridging mechanism between the public and private persona. They have a different set of challenges that are analogues to those of the individual donor. How open a shop do we run? Is this an old girl–old boy network, or are we reaching out to new constituencies in the community? Do we invite recipient organizations into the policy decisions around program and allocation? Do we invite young people onto the board? Does our board really reflect the diversity of the community? Are we going to be an asset-accumulation organization or a donor-service organization? Is our understanding of the systemic issues facing the community deep enough? Is our grant-making strategically relevant?

The challenge of connectedness

If the United States is in a crisis of civic engagement and if the role of philanthropy is that of providing one important bridge, what are the new ideas and the innovations that promote connectedness?

In Washington, D.C., entrepreneur Mario Marino has put together a youth social venture fund and raised more than $30 million to invest in Capital Region programs working with children. His staff consists of three highly qualified management consultants whose job is to work with the organizations funded.

New hybrid organizations, part intermediary and part consultant, like New Profit, Inc. and the Entrepreneurs' Foundation, are bridging e-economy wealth to philanthropy. In Boston, Boston Jewish Venture Partners is forming to raise $10 million to invest over seven years in a combination of Jewish and civic issues. In Seattle, Social Venture Partners now has 250 partners and is beginning to expand and enrich its educational programs for donor investors. The New Ventures in Philanthropy initiative of the Forum of Regional Associations of Grantmakers has now supported twenty-five regional efforts to promote giving. One of the sites, Giving New England, has chosen the learning and giving circle as its primary platform for growth. The concept of the philanthropic advisory service is being increasingly considered as a fringe benefit with new-wealth companies.

The media are on the case. From *Time* magazine to *Fast Company*, the buzz around wealth keeps turning toward philanthropy. And sometimes they even get it right. Organizations like the Museum of Science in Boston and the New England Aquarium have developed learning circles around programmatic themes of interest to their supporters.

In a learning and giving circle, a group of donors or volunteers pools resources and then collectively determines where and how they are to be deployed. The giving circle's earlier analogue is the investment clubs of the 1950s and 1960s, where participants learned how to buy and sell stocks. These circles are a form of introductory course on philanthropy, and ultimately the learning circles back to the participant's own approach to giving.

Thus, a new donor is launched, but in the company of others. We all know loners and joiners, and one of the interesting things about these circles is that they are attracting many who by instinct are loners into a far more public process. There is the potential that this phenomenon will produce donors who are prepared and able to move further along the path, who will more readily understand the transformation of self into a member of the polis and the larger world.

And still more challenges

How many more challenges are there? Many, many, including the challenge to think globally and the challenge of time.

We started out with bridges, dialogue, and the realization that this was, for all of us, a journey. In this journey, the dialogue is both internal and external. Although I have touched on some of the challenges in that journey, this chapter has not begun to address those issues within ourselves and within society that are the true challenges.

Here are some of the bridges that stand between the private and the public persona, between the self and the larger world:

Internal Bridges

From ambition to acceptance
From ego to sharing
From fear to love
From pragmatic to poetic
From materiality to spirituality
From obsession to perspective
From hyperaction to contemplation
From passive to active
From dominance to yielding
From being alone to belonging

External Bridges

From self to community
From community to community

From haves to have-nots
From one race to another
From prejudice to tolerance
From confrontation to reconciliation
From violence to peace
From ignorance to knowledge

I end with my poem that addresses the one factor that will determine whether we rise to meet these challenges and whether the philanthropic manifest destiny we all want can be realized. It is a matter of will, and that is the name of the poem.

Will

It's a matter of will
This game of life
is inner rather than outer

conception is nice
but doesn't express will
while execution oh yes

no prescriptions here
yet focus drives
closure

organizations are built
survive and prosper
based on will one or multiple

governments fail from lack
fortunes rise and fall
and great art is made by force of

you won't find will in résumés
it isn't always noisy
and often lies deep

obsession while not will
is part of the intensity
which is a precondition

the ah ha components are
passion and huge ambition
all over a good idea

will unromanticized
along with love
it is our most powerful

References

Remmer, E. *What's a Donor to Do? The State of Donor Resources in America Today.* Boston: The Philanthropic Initiative, 2000.

Yankelovich, D. *The Magic of Dialogue: Transforming Conflict into Cooperation.* New York: Simon & Schuster, 1999.

Ylvisaker, P.N. *Small Can Be Effective.* Washington, D.C.: Council on Foundations, 1989.

H. PETER KAROFF *is founder and chairman of The Philanthropic Initiative, Inc.*

Index

Abkhaz Republic, 85
Acknowledgment of donors. *See* Recognition
Aetna, 71
African Americans, 72
Altruist donor type, 64
Ambition, donor, 91–92
America Online, 90–91
American Association of Fundraising Counsel Trust for Philanthropy, 11
America's Promise, 91
Appreciated property, 44
Aristotle, 30
Asian donors, 73
Assets: appreciated property as, 44; liquidation of, 45–46; and price effects, 44; of small business owners, 45–46; types of, 35; wealth effect on, 47; and wealth transfer, 34–36
Association with others, 21–22, 28
Avery, R., 10

Bankers Trust Private Banking, 27
Barnes, R. C., 55
Baumeister, R. F., 51–52, 55, 63, 65, 66
Beavin, J. H., 56
Behavioral effects, 40–48
Berger, P. L., 66
Board of Governors of the Federal Reserve, 15n.3
Boston College Wealth Transfer Microsimulation Model (WTMM), 9–10, 12
Boston Jewish Venture Partners, 93
Boston National Association for the Advancement of Colored People, 86
Bray, T. J., 28
Bruner, J., 66

Bush, G. W., 71
Business 2.0, 69

Campbell, C., 53
Carson, E. D., 69, 73, 76
Chambers, R., 91
Charitable bequests: current economic distribution of, 9; from estates, 9, 12–13; to heirs, 9, 14, 27; projected economic distributions of, 12–13; and taxes, 9, 14, 26–29
Charitable giving: of African Americans, 72; of Asian donors, 73; and decision-making process of donors, 24–26; and donor motivation, 18–23, 52, 61–65, 66; and donor stages, 83–84; and donors of color, 72–77; economic distribution of, 8–9, 34t; effect of taxes on, 14, 40–41, 42–44, 46–48; and feedback to donors, 59, 62; gift process of, 82; and importance of donor choice, 25–26, 30; inter vivos, 8–9, 11–12; and intrinsic meaning, 52, 61–65, 66; liquidating effect on, 45–46; patterns of, 8–9, 34t; and price effects, 44; projected estimates of, 11–13; and relationship to wealth, 14–15; and religion, 23; and repeal of estate tax, 26–29; and social networks, 21–22; and supply-side effects, 13–15; systemic issues of, 89, 92; wealth effect on, 46–48
Chenault, K., 73
Cialdini, R. B., 54
Communitarian donor type, 63–64
Confucianism, 72–73
Content of information, 56, 57, 61
Conventions, presidential nominating, 70
Corporations, Subchapter S, 46

97

Back Issue/Subscription Order Form

Copy or detach and send to:
Jossey-Bass, 989 Market Street, San Francisco, CA 94103-1741

Call or fax toll free!
Phone 888-378-2537 6AM-5PM PST; Fax 800-605-2665

Back issues: Please send me the following issues at $28 each
(Important: please include series initials and issue number, such as PF10)

1. PF _____

_____

_____

$ _____ Total for single issues

$ _____ Shipping charges (for single issues *only;* subscriptions are exempt from shipping charges): Up to $30, add $5^{50} • $30^{01}–$50, add $6^{50} $50^{01}–$75, add $8 • $75^{01}–$100, add $10 • $100^{01}–$150, add $12 Over $150, call for shipping charge

Subscriptions Please ❏ start ❏ renew my subscription to *New Directions for Philanthropic Fundraising* at the following rate:

US:	❏ Individual $75	❏ Institutional $147
Canada:	❏ Individual $75	❏ Institutional $187
All others:	❏ Individual $99	❏ Institutional $221

NOTE: Issues are published quarterly. Subscriptions are for the calendar year only. Subscriptions begin with the Spring issue. Add appropriate sales tax for your state for single issue orders. No sales tax for U.S. subscriptions.

$ _____ Total single issues and subscriptions (Canadian residents, add GST for subscriptions and single issues)

❏ Payment enclosed (U.S. check or money order only)

❏ VISA, MC, AmEx, Discover Card # _____ Exp. date _____

Signature _____ Day phone _____

❏ Bill me (U.S. institutional orders only. Purchase order required)

Purchase order # _____

Federal Tax ID 135593032   GST 89102-8052

Name _____

Address _____

_____

Phone _____ E-mail _____

For more information about Jossey-Bass, visit our Web site at:
www.josseybass.com   **PRIORITY CODE = ND1**

Previous Issues Available